FROM HIRING TO FIRING

A Practical Guide to Selecting, Motivating, and Retaining the Best Employees

Robert E. Ledman
Sarah Popowski

Hamilton Books
A member of
The Rowman & Littlefield Publishing Group
Lanham · Boulder · New York · Toronto · Plymouth, UK

Copyright © 2007 by
Hamilton Books
4501 Forbes Boulevard
Suite 200
Lanham, Maryland 20706
Hamilton Books Acquisitions Department (301) 459-3366

Estover Road
Plymouth PL6 7PY
United Kingdom

Library of Congress Control Number: 2006932009
ISBN-13: 978-0-7618-3609-4 (paperback : alk. paper)
ISBN-10: 0-7618-3609-8 (paperback : alk. paper)

For my wife and best friend Shira for her support and encouragement

This is dedicated to my mother, Paula Popowski, who I always try to emulate. The greatest compliment I am given is that I am just like her.

TABLE OF CONTENTS

Chapter 1   Recruiting and Selecting the Best Candidate   1
Chapter 2   Preparing the New Employee for the Job   11
Chapter 3   Communicating Effectively to   17
             Ensure Understanding
Chapter 4   Leading Effective Employees   25
Chapter 5   Motivating People by Meeting Their Needs   33
Chapter 6   Reinforcing Behavior and Providing Feedback   43
Chapter 7   How Do I Know They Are Doing a Good Job   51
Chapter 8   Monitoring and Documenting Performance   57
Chapter 9   Reviewing Performance for Improvement   63
             and Development
Chapter 10   What if the Employee is Not Performing   71

PREFACE

This guide should be useful to people who have recently been promoted to their first management position and those who are anticipating their first management job. It provides specific guidance for dealing with a myriad of management challenges.

This book tries to distill substantial content from a typical undergraduate course in management into a short, practical, easily read guide for new managers. We recognize that there are many areas of management we could present that are not mentioned in this volume. Our intent is to provide an overview of the tasks of managers as they relate specifically to the employees in the manager's unit. Topics such as organizing the work unit, managing teams, unit cohesion, and many others are intentionally not included in order to maintain the focus of the book.

The book is organized in a sequence to take the reader from hiring employees through managing the employees' performance to taking corrective actions up to and including firing. Each chapter stands alone as a complete topic so the reader can pick the order he or she wants to read them in. We have ordered them in a sequence that makes sense to us, based on our experience as managers.

Due to the nature of management as an art and a science there are sometimes distinctive differences from chapter to chapter. Some chapters present very specific actions to take and suggest ways to successfully complete them. Other chapters are less concrete because there are no specific actions that can be spelled out that will work in most situations. Those chapters present the material in a partially theoretic framework with practical suggestions and examples to illustrate the concepts.

We are confident that any manager who uses the ideas and suggestions in this book will be successful in optimizing the performance of the employees who report to them. We sincerely believe those managers who practice and become proficient at the actions and behaviors we describe should have the respect and commitment of their employees to do their best work.

Robert E. Ledman
Sarah Popowski
Atlanta, GA
2006

Chapter 1
Recruiting and Selecting the Best Candidates

Perhaps the most important job of a manager is getting the right people on the team. The people selected will determine your ultimate success as a manager, making it a part of your job that should be taken the most seriously. A good choice can add energy and motivate your team to perform at a higher level than before. A poor choice can bring the team down, de-motivate them and impact productivity. "One bad apple can spoil the whole bunch" is never more true than when looking at whom you are going to select to join your group.

There are very legitimate reasons to have openings in your department. Some of these might be:

- Resignations
- Termination
- Newly created position
- Employee not returning from a leave of absence
- Temporary need of the department (use of contract and/or temporary help)

Regardless of the reason for the open position, a manager should always make certain that he or she gets the "right" person vs. "a" person. Ask any manager who has panicked when a position has been open for what is believed "too long" and hired someone just to fill the opening. The individual hired is not the best fit but filled the void in the department. In most of these situations, the manager will probably tell you that the hiring of that person was a mistake and did not work out. The person may have been technically competent but did not fit in with the culture and dynamics of the organization or department. In most cases, the person either quits because of job dissatisfaction or has performance or behavioral issues that lead to termination.

This chapter will address some important considerations in recruiting and selecting the "best" and the "right" candidates.

THE IMPORTANCE OF FIT

Southwest Airlines, one of the most profitable airlines in the history of aviation, has a very simple approach to the way it selects people to be part of their team. "Hire for attitude, train for skill" is the mantra for Southwest's hiring. You can always bring someone in at a certain skill level and enhance that skill. If the best candidate has all the skills needed but may not have the best demeanor or attitude, consider the alternatives before hiring him or her. You will get the skills but you may also get a lot of aggravation, upset the chemistry of the team and effect morale.

If you have a particular task that needs to be done and you find someone that has these skills at a level of high proficiency, logic may tell you that you have found your new employee. However, unless the person will be working in a vacuum, he or she will have to interact with others. Will they likely need others to personally be successful and assure the success of the team? If the preceding is true then skills will not be enough.

Many managers do not consider attitude and fit when recruiting and selecting candidates. Typically, they will rely solely on skills that a person can bring to the job. Follow the Southwest mantra, "hire for attitude, train for skill" and you will very rarely go wrong. The reason is that you can always enhance the skills of someone. However, if you have identified someone who may not have the attitude you want, do not think you will be able to change it. It just doesn't happen. One of the authors once participated in a panel at a career fair. She was asked what candidate she would rather have – someone who has 100% of the skills needed, but a poor attitude and thus not a good fit OR someone who has 80% of the skills needed but had the right attitude and was a good fit for the team and the organization. Without hesitation, the latter is the preferred candidate.

It should be understood that there must be a minimum skill set for the job. The best attitude and fit will not make up for not having some level of proficiency. The point being made here is a manager should never think that an attitude can be changed once a person is on the job. It will not happen. So take time and hold out for the best overall fit.

KNOW WHAT YOU WANT

When you have an open position on your team, many times the first instinct is to fill the position quickly. You are down in staff. The workload and organizational expectations are not sympathetic to your situation. So, it is only natural that panic sets in.

Rather than panic, an opening in your department can, and often should, also be looked at as an opportunity to assess where you are and where you need to be. It is a time to reflect on the skills of your team that brought you to a certain point and the skills you will need to go to another level of performance. As people have been added to your team so has the total skill set of the team.

Take a close look at the job that is now vacant. For the person who left, what skills and attributes did he/she have that brought success? Also, conversely, what skills and attributes did this person lack or not develop to help move your department forward to achieve its goals and objectives? What skills and abilities are needed to fill gaps in the team's skill and competency set?

A way to help you assess your current and future needs is to perform a job analysis. It is helpful to begin a job analysis prior to someone leaving a position to get a handle on the "what is" (i.e. the current tasks and competencies needed to do the job). Job analysis is discussed further in Chapter 7.

The following is a table you can be use to help you assess the current requirements as well as future requirements of the job.

Position: _____
Reports To: _____

Skill	Competency Needed to Perform Skill	Behaviors Needed for Success	Other Factors for Success

Skill – Before moving forward on hiring for a position, it is a good idea to ask yourself and others who can give constructive feedback on what is needed in this position to assure the success of the individual and the team. Computer skills are common for many positions today. What must this position have for success (i.e. word processing, spreadsheet, presentation)? Earlier it was mentioned that you should hire attitude and train for skill. Having a minimum skill level is not a contradiction of hire for attitude, train for skill. You must have a minimum skill set defined before evaluating a candidate for the position.

Competency –Using the example of computer skills, the candidate has experience in the applications you need (i.e. word processing, spreadsheet, and presentation). But having worked with an application is one thing. Having the competency to do what you need may be another. Word processing is a good example. A candidate may have a level of skill in word processing. Perhaps he/she has created documents, edited, etc. But you may need competency in other areas such as mail merge, table set up, use and insertion of illustrations. So determine the competency needed in a skill.

Behaviors – In addition to skills and competencies, it is important to look at the behaviors needed to assure success in a position. Behaviors may include things like customer service, communication, etc. These are separated from skills as one's tendency in these areas may have more to do with attitude than skill. In customer service, you can do all the training in the world but if someone does not have the right attitude, all the skill in the world will not help you achieve your success. So, look at what behaviors/attitudes are essential for you and your team to be successful.

Other Factors for Success – This is a "catch all" category for those things that may not fit in skills, competencies and behaviors. Examples of these can be things that may not be essential for the job but can add value. For example if you are hiring for a financial position, an added value is someone with enough presentation skills to explain reports and results to a non financial audience. While it may not be a deal breaker in hiring someone, it can add value to your team.

Once you have completed a job analysis, it is a good idea to review the job description if it is an existing position. Make the necessary revisions to help you have clarity on what your need. If it is a new position, this will help you develop the job description for posting and advertising.

Some think the job description is a tool that Human Resources Departments use to drive managers crazy. Some see it as additional work and not necessary. It is important for several reasons.

First, it helps you get on paper what the important elements of the job are. These include things like the position title, who the position reports to, what department the position resides in, and a summary of the position. While this may sound simple, getting these things on paper develops clarity of the position. Clarity not just for you as a manager, but also it gives clarity to others inside and outside the organization about the position.

A job description should also include essential duties and responsibilities. These should be kept broad. By keeping them broad, you minimize the need to constantly update. Also, by keeping them broad, you don't have a five page list of essential duties and responsibilities. So, what happens when you need to have an employee do something outside the scope of the job description? Any job description should have some statement that says the job description is not all inclusive. An example might be: "The above duties and responsibilities describe the general nature of work for employees in this position, but this is not intended as an exclusive or all inclusive inventory of all duties required of employees in this job."

Another reason the job description is helpful is it clarifies the qualifications needed for the position such as type of education, work experience and skills needed. Having these and other elements in the job description helps you clarify and explain the position.

From the Human Resource perspective, it clarifies how this person will be paid (hourly or salary), and what the physical and mental requirements are (included since the Americans with Disabilities Act was passed). An example of a job description is shown on the following page. This topic will be discussed again from a different perspective in Chapter 7.

Now that you have completed the job analysis and job description, you are ready to recruit.

HAVE A PLAN

To make the hiring process go as smoothly as possible, you should have a plan in place. This can include:

- Where to advertise
- With whom to network (who to tell that you have a position open)
- Who will screen candidates
- Who will interview/participate in face to face interviews with the candidate

You should not have to do this alone. Collaborate with your Human Resources Department or professional in your organization.

Sample Job Description

JOB DESCRIPTION
POSITION TITLE: Administrative Assistant   **FLSA**: Non-Exempt
DEPARTMENT: Marketing   **POSITION NO.** 100.105
REPORTS TO: Department Director

PRINCIPAL FUNCTION: Under supervision of department director provide administrative support to the Marketing Department, working with professional staff at all levels, planning and organizing diversified workload to facilitate administrative operations in the division and/or department.

ESSENTIAL DUTIES AND RESPONSIBILITIES:

1. Organize and prioritize assigned work, according to established guidelines, compiling and entering information on donor database, maintaining records, creating and filing documents, correspondence, mailings, faxes, spreadsheets and packets, proofreading to ensure production of clear and accurate documents and records.
2. Assist in the coordination of events and meetings related to assigned area, including invitations, coordination of facilities and food, calendar notices, agendas, and other materials as needed to guarantee complete preparations for scheduled activities.
3. Initiate and respond to requests and questions from co-workers and others in the organization according to procedures to facilitate effective communications department and the organization.
4. Assist with special projects, researching and preparing drafts of requested information to provide professional staff with necessary data.
5. Function as a member of administrative team, providing support as requested or assigned.
6. Promote the mission of the organization at all times through superior customer service to all and through the efficient use and care of all resources.

The above job duties and responsibilities describe the general nature and level of work for employees in this position, but this is not intended as an exclusive or all-inclusive inventory of all duties required of employees in this job.

STATUS AND SCOPE: No supervisory responsibilities. Initiate and respond to ongoing contacts with department staff, other department staff and customers.

QUALIFICATIONS: High school diploma with two years administrative assistant experience or Bachelor's degree and one year administrative experience. Demonstrated written and verbal communication skills, PC and database skills, time management, event planning and customer service abilities.

PHYSICAL REQUIREMENTS: Intermittent standing, walking and sitting for extended periods of time working at computer. Must be able to read computer screen for accurate production of documents and spreadsheets and to use telephone and switchboard equipment. Occasionally, lift up to 20 lbs. of materials and set up tables and chairs for events.

MENTAL REQUIREMENTS: Work in open area with frequent interruptions and distractions. Must be able to prioritize and complete multiple, competing tasks accurately with careful attention to detail and function as a member of administrative team.

Employee Signature:_____**Date:** _____

Employee Name (Print): _____

Authorized   **by:**
_____

Title: _____**Date:** _____

POWER OF THE TELEPONE INTERVIEW

After reviewing resumes and identifying prospective candidates that interest you, a good next step is to have a conversation on the telephone with those candidates. This can be done by you as the manager who is doing the hiring for the position, someone in your department to whom you have delegated the responsibility or Human Resources. You should be sure you are consistent in having the same questions asked of all candidates you screen on the phone. Also, have a copy of the job description handy to explain the primary responsibilities of the job.

Below are some questions that can be useful in a phone interview:

1. Why do you feel you are qualified for the job (after having heard the

primary responsibilities of the job)?
2. Why are you looking to make a change?
3. Why does the potential for working for our company interest you?
4. What did you like most about your most recent position?
5. What did you like least about you most recent position?

You will be surprised by what you can glean from a telephone interview. Here are some things to look for:

- How articulate is the person?
- How are the questions answered?
- How does the candidate speak of current and/or former employers?

Of those whom you interviewed on the phone, who impressed you enough to go to the next step – the face to face interview? By doing the phone interviews, you have saved yourself time by not bringing everyone who looks good on paper for a face to face interview.

THE FACE TO FACE INTEVIEW

One decision to make when bringing a candidate in is with whom he/she will meet. Here you need to see how your organization interviews candidates. Be sure to follow the procedures of your organization, if any, so no one will be left out. For example, your supervisor may want to meet any candidate for a position in your department. Also, including members of your department in the interviewing process can be very beneficial in candidate selection.

Those whom you may want to consider including are people who will be colleagues of the position for which you are hiring. They probably will be working more closely with the person being hired than you. So, having "buy in" from others already in the department can play a huge role in how successful the new team member will be. Those interviewing the candidate also will have a vested interest in the success of the new team member. Also, your current team members can be more patient if it takes longer than you would like to fill the position as they would not want just anyone. They will be willing to take on the additional workload to wait for the right person. If members of your team are not included, they may not be as vested in the person you choose.

On the flip side, don't get carried away and include everyone. This can be overwhelming to the candidate. Be inclusive, if appropriate, but also be selective.

Once you have selected the interviewing team, a next step can be deciding on what questions to ask. It is important that you partner closely with your Human Resources colleague to be sure the questions you do ask are not discriminatory in any manner.

There are different types of questions you can formulate for the interview. There are the technical questions that address the skill level of a candidate. An example would be to inquire about and/or test computer skills necessary for the job (i.e. word processing, spreadsheet, etc.). Another type of question to ask is what is called the behavioral question. These questions can provide insight into how a candidate may respond in certain situations. The following are examples of behavioral questions:

1. What do you consider one of your greatest work accomplishments and why?
2. Tell me a time when you had a conflict with a fellow employee or supervisor. What was it and how did you resolve it?
3. What was the most significant or difficult problem you encountered on a job? How did you approach it? What did you actually do?
4. Describe a situation where you had to build trust with another individual or group. What did you do? Was it successful? What indicated it was successful?

Now you are ready to actually conduct the interview. To best assess the candidates, it is a good idea to use the same questions for each candidate. It will give you a far more objective view of each candidate. Here, consistency in conducting each interview makes it easier to make good decisions as to who is best qualified and will be the best fit for your organization. You should also consider having at least one other person (a colleague) participate in the interview with you so you can compare perceptions of each candidate after the interview.

MAKING YOUR FINAL SELECTION

You have interviewed the candidates. You have your notes from the questions you asked. It is time to make the decision. Now is the time to partner with those who were part of the interviewing process.

There are a couple of approaches you may want to take in partnering in this decision. One is to use a rating sheet that each interviewer completes after meeting with a candidate. You can rate things such as technical competence, attitude, fit for the team. On the following page is an example of a rating sheet that can be used.

You probably have formed an opinion as to who you think the best candidate is. Remember, the team of interviewers has also formed opinions. It is important to listen to their feedback and take it into consideration when making your final decision. More often than not, you will be on the same page as to what candidate is the best one for the position. That will make your decision easy.

In some instances, you may find that you and your team of interviewers may not come to the same conclusion. In this case, take the feedback you have been given, but the ultimate decision is yours. The person to whom you directly report may need to be consulted or included. Check your employer's policies.

All along the way, your Human Resources department should be kept abreast of where you are in the process. You should know what needs to be done before an offer can be extended. Things like reference checks and background checks, if used, need to be coordinated.

Another important element is salary. This is a touchy issue for you as a supervisor, and the potential candidate. Each wants to keep options open and negotiate as well as possible. But you do need to know if you are at least in the same ballpark. Regardless, some candidates will be reluctant to give a figure. One way you may want to get a sense of the candidate's expectation is to ask for a range instead of a specific amount. Some may be more comfortable doing that than giving a specific amount. How much you can pay is dependent on how much is budgeted for the position and/or the salary range determined by your Human Resources Department. Typically, exceptions to a range must have approval from another source – your direct supervisor, finance, human resources.

Interview Rating Sheet

Candidate: _____

Position: _____

Interviewer _____

Please rate each item from 1 – 5 (5 being excellent).

Technical competence   _____

Attitude   _____

Ability to relate to others/develop relationships _____

Verbal communication skills   _____

Presentation   _____

Comments:

It is possible you will find someone who is willing to accept less than your lowest end of a salary range. You may think you are getting a real steal. But remember, it is important to be fair as well.

You need to know the procedure for offers being extended in your organization. Sometimes it will be Human Resources. Oftentimes, it will be the hiring manager. If you are the one who will be extending the offer, you will need to be equipped with other information besides salary. You will need to know the benefits package. This may include health and dental benefits, vacation, retirement plans, etc. The human resources department should have information on this.

When you extend the offer, be very specific. For example, say something like "I would like to offer you the position of administrative assistant at a starting salary of $_____. In addition you will be eligible for full benefits as provided. I am excited about the prospect of you becoming a part of our team."

The candidate may want some time to think about the offer. If so, set a specific date and time that you should hear back (i.e. no later than the end of the day Wednesday).

Once a candidate accepts the offer, he or she may request an offer letter. Let your human resources department professional handle this. There is specific language that should be used.

SUMMARY

Recruiting and selecting the best candidates is a very important part of being a supervisor. The people you select as part of your team will determine your success in your position. Think it through, find the best person, and don't look to fill the void with "a person".

By following a structured thoughtful process, you will make a better decision, assuring the success of your team and ultimately, your organization.

TO DO LIST

- For one of the positions you supervise, prepare a job description from scratch based on a job analysis using the table provided in this chapter.
- For the position you just analyzed, write a hiring plan.
- Make a list of the criteria you will use to screen applicants before the telephone interview.
- For the positions in your department, create a set of criteria for choosing who you will ask to assist with face-to-face interviews.
- Practice writing interview questions that are job specific and are intended to help you assess a candidate's skills and abilities.

Chapter 2
Preparing the New Employee for the Job

Once you have offered a candidate a job and it has been accepted, your work to orient the new member of your team begins. Some may think *I don't have to worry about anything until he/she shows up on their first day of work.* Nothing can be further from the truth. The time to begin orienting a new employee begins before they walk in the door—not the day they show up.

In this chapter, you will learn some approaches to preparing new employees to be successful in your organization.

BEFORE YOUR EMPLOYEE BEGINS

The orientation work begins before your employee starts the job. Once you have agreed on a start date with the employee, you should start the orientation process. Think of your new employee as a customer. One of the keys to successful customer service is meeting or exceeding your customer's expectations. The same should be true when your new employee begins at your organization. Making a good first impression is a positive step to having a satisfied, productive employee.

The list below identifies some things that should be done in advance of the employee beginning in your organization.

1. Inform appropriate staff by announcing the new employee and his or her start date. This can be done via email. Regardless of the method used, you want the new employee to know that others know they are coming.
2. Identify office/work space. When the employee arrives on the first day is not the time to be figuring this out.
3. Secure any necessary furnishings. You identified the office/work space, now set it up with the appropriate furnishings (desk, chair, basic office supplies such as tape dispenser, stapler, etc.).
4. Install a telephone with an extension assigned and programmed. The extension, if any; the direct number if applicable, etc.
5. Order business cards, if appropriate for position. To be complete, you will need the information such as phone number (see above),

appropriate fax number, email address and other relevant information for the position.

6. Set up a computer and passwords as needed. Be sure there is a password assigned that your new employee can use to log into the system and can be changed. The computer will allow them to work from the very first day.

7. Identify key people with whom the new employee is to meet. This may be the last on the list but perhaps most important. Who are the key people your new employee should meet/have face time with soon after they begin? Think this through and be as thorough as possible, but not too overwhelming. An obvious meeting is with Human Resources to assure all paperwork is completed for payroll/benefits purposes. Your organization may accomplish this in one of two ways. There may be a general orientation session of multiple new employees, or an individual meeting with your new employee. Other key people to consider are perhaps your direct supervisor and those in other departments on whom your new employee will depend for assistance to be successful. Also, depending on the size of your organization, you may want to consider meeting with the person who heads the organization (CEO, President, etc.). For someone just starting with the organization, it is important that they know the names and can recognize key individuals in the organization. The form on the next page may be helpful for you to use as a tool when scheduling appointments. They do not all have to happen the first day.

8. Those whom the new employee meets will vary depending on how your organization is structured. Use this as a guide to develop those things you want to be sure are done. Add or delete from these suggestions to make it unique for your organization. As a supervisor, you may delegate these responsibilities to a member of your team. The important thing is to get it done before your new employee appears at your door.

THE EMPLOYEE'S FIRST DAY

As previously mentioned, your organization may have a unique way of handling an employee's first day(s) on the job. In larger organizations, your human resources department may have structured orientations to accommodate a group of employees at one time. This can handle many of the generic things an employee may have to do regardless of position. These include such things as getting identification (ID) badges made, getting an overview of the organization (mission, vision, values), touring of the facility, reviewing safety and security issues, completing paperwork (payroll, benefits, employee handbook, etc.). Check with your Human Resources Department to see who is responsible for assuring these items are completed.

If your organization has such a structured program, the employee's first day may be taken care of. You may not even see the employee on the first day. They may report to you on the second or third day depending on the length of the general orientation.

Appointment Schedule

Employee Name: _____

Date of Hire: _____

Position: _____

Department: _____

Name/Dept.	Title	Date of Appt.	Time	Location

If your organization does not have a general orientation for a group of employees, you may be responsible for the first day of employment and the items above (i.e. ID badges, overview of the organization, etc.) may be your responsibility as a supervisor. Regardless, there are some things you should do when the employee is with you on the first day.

1. Welcome Sign. A nice touch is to have some type of welcome sign in the general area where the employee will be working. This can include name, title and department. It is also a way to inform employees in other departments that someone new has started, and to seek them out.

2. Introduce Employees to Fellow Team Members. When the employee reports to you for work, one of the first things you should do is introduce them to the members of the team. Remember, your current staff should already be anticipating the arrival of the new team member. Now they get to formally meet. Give them an opportunity to have brief conversations and let them know they will have more time later to get to know one another.

3. Assign a Co-Worker to be a Contact for New Employee. In addition to you, consider assigning the new employee to a colleague whom can help them *learn the ropes* about the organization. This can be the *go to* person in your absence. Be selective in whom you choose. Choose someone who is positive and will be upbeat about the organization and the department.

4. Ensure that the New Employee has Lunch Plans. Be sure your new employee has lunch with someone on the team. This can either be you or someone you assign. If you assign someone to take your new employee to lunch, be sure it is someone who is positive and upbeat about their job and the organization. The last thing you want is to have someone who is negative and down on the organization to share that with a new team member.

5. Review the Job Description and Have the Employee Sign it. This is an important thing to do. You may have reviewed the job description when the employee was interviewing. It is important to go over again now that they are part of the team. This will give you the opportunity to review the essential duties and responsibilities and answer questions. It can also be a framework to articulate your expectations. Be certain the employee understands the content of the job description and you have answered any questions before they are asked to sign.

6. Answer Employee's Questions and Confirm Work Plans for the First Week. Be sure you have assignments for your new employee when they arrive. One of the worst things you can do is hire someone and then not know how you are going to keep them occupied. Go over the work assignment and be certain your new employee understands the assignment and has resources to go to for questions and/or further clarification. The *go to* person may be you. Regardless, make certain that they know whom to go to.

THE FIRST SEVERAL WEEKS

As your new employee becomes more acclimated in the new surroundings of your organization, it is a good idea to keep close tabs on him or her. If anything, over manage vs. under manage during this time. You will be learning work styles and he or she will be learning more about your expectations. You are also using this time to "teach" them their job and your expectations.

Below are two things you can consider doing to keep the close communication going during the first few weeks:

1. Check in each day or every other day. This is nothing formal. Check on how things are going; ask if the assignment(s) being worked on are moving forward in a comfortable manner. Ask questions to reassure yourself that they understand the tasks you have assigned. This can be a 30 second conversation, but keeps you in touch.

2. Have a formal meeting each week. This should be ongoing but particularly crucial in the first several weeks. These meetings have the goal of reviewing the assignments being worked on to assure the new employee that what is

being done aligns with your expectations. As you become more comfortable with the work being done, continue to have these meetings. The frequency can be based on your comfort level, corporate culture, or the need of the employee. A recommended minimum is every two weeks.

Also very important during the first several weeks is to assure that your new employee has met various people in the organization. An appointment sheet was shown previously in this chapter. Ask your new employee to report on the progress in meeting people. If there are some meetings that have not taken place and are particularly important to the success of the employee, there may need to be some intervention on your part.

In the first few weeks, the most important thing to remember as a supervisor is to check in with the employee, formally and informally. Nothing breeds success more than communication. Constant communication helps your new employee become acclimated more quickly to the job. It also shows support and your investment in the success of your new team member. Equally important for the supervisor is providing feedback to the employee, and recognizing when they are gaining the confidence and capability to function with less direct oversight. See chapter 6.

The following identifies other things that you may want to consider that will enhance your new employee's experience in the first few weeks:

1. Assign a mentor. This can be someone in or outside your department. The mentor serves as someone who will help the employee navigate the organization, learn about other departments, and be an advisor. Mentoring can be a win/win for the employee and the organization. A mentor is one from whom the new employee can learn and grow in the position and the organization. Take time to choose the right person.

2. Give the new employee a schedule of important meetings, programs, etc. that he or she will need to attend. These can be things like client meetings, department meetings, all staff meetings, etc.

3. Recognize the new employee at meetings he/she is attending and communicate how happy you are to have him/her on your team. No one ever has *overdosed* on too much recognition.

There are some that may question whether all of this is necessary. As with an external customer, however, you never have a second chance to make a first impression. The first days/weeks of a new employee's tenure with the organization can form a long lasting impression of the culture of your organization. In addition, it contributes to the employee's success learning the job and the expectations. That will likely result in lower turnover.

TO DO LIST

- Prepare a Checklist of things to do before each new employee begins.
    - o Learn what is necessary in your organization
- Make a list of the people new employees should meet in their first day and their first week.
- Write a schedule for a new employee's first day.
- Write a schedule and plan for keeping close and frequent contact with the employee in the first several weeks.

Chapter 3
Communicating Effectively to Ensure Understanding

The previous chapters made mention of communication in several places. Communication is something people at work do regularly. However, they may not be doing it well. Good communication is essential for supervisors and managers to be successful in any efforts to train or maximize performance of employees. If the manager does not communicate effectively, the employees will not have a clear understanding of their job duties, assigned tasks, or expectations. This chapter will discuss how to make communication more effective. To understand communication, it is necessary to begin with some theoretical discussion.

Communication is only effective if it accomplishes its purpose. Good communication requires the ability to present one's message effectively and have it received as it was intended. There are specific skills that can improve managers' ability to present, or send, their message and their ability to effectively receive the message for better understanding. This chapter will discuss the basic communication model and things the senders and receivers can do to increase the likelihood of each party having the same understanding of the intended message. Underlying all of our communication is the presence of non-verbal cues. Some estimates suggest that as much as ninety percent of communication is non-verbal.

A COMMUNICATIONS MODEL

Communication is the process of sending and receiving messages through appropriate channels as shown in the model on the following page. As illustrated in this model the sender encodes the message into words and/or symbols and sends the message through a communication channel to the receiver. The receiver decodes the message and through feedback, either verbal or non-verbal, indicates his or her understanding. During this entire process there is potential interference known as noise. This interference is present in many forms but the term noise is used to indicate anything that hinders clear communication. This model contains four components—sending, receiving,

channels, and noise—that will be considered individually. The feedback
component will be considered primarily in the discussion of receiving.

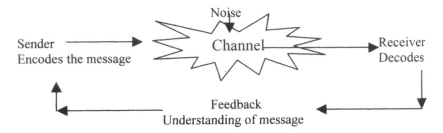

SENDING COMMUNICATION

The sender, as the starting point in the communication process, plays a
crucial role in its success. The sender must strive to encode their message in a
clear and concise manner to facilitate understanding by the receiver. Here are
several steps senders can take to increase the chances their message will be
correctly understood. Perhaps the most important thing the sender can do is use
the most precise language possible. For example, one can ask the question
"Could you complete this project for me?" and receive an answer of yes. Two
weeks later the project has not been completed. Why? The question asked if
someone *could* finish the project, which asked about the employee's skill rather
than his or her willingness to finish the project. Admittedly this is not likely to
happen, but it does illustrate the importance of precision. Another area where
precision is important is in grammatical form. A sentence can take on different
meaning based on the grammatical structure and punctuation of the sentence.

The following example should help make this point. Consider the meaning of
the two sentences given here. Are they the same?
1.   With headquarters in Santa Clara, California, NUMMI builds Toyotas and
     Chevrolets in a joint venture of the two companies.
2.   In a joint venture of the two companies, NUMMI builds Toyotas and
     Chevrolets with headquarters in Santa Clara, California.

Even though the same words are used, the two sentences have different
meanings. The second sentence implies that Toyotas and Chevrolets have
headquarters in Santa Clara. The second sentence is also not as clear about what
companies make up the joint venture.

In oral communication the ability to clearly enunciate and properly
pronounce words is essential to understanding. Regional accents often contribute
to variations in pronunciations and the speed with which one speaks may impact
the enunciation. We are all familiar with the "pak your cah" of Boston or "y'all"
in the south as an example of a regional accent that can interfere with the clarity
of the message. Intonation and inflection are closely related to pronunciation.
Anyone who has heard the famous I Had a Dream speech of Dr. Martin Luther

King, Jr. probably noticed the rhythm and cadence of that very moving speech. Dr. King was a master of inflection; he knew just when to soften his voice or speak louder to hold the listeners attention. Presidents Reagan and Clinton are often cited for their oratory skills. Both of them understood the importance of intonation. They understood the importance of emphasizing important points with the right tone of voice. Mr. Reagan's famous command to Russian President Gorbachev to "Tear down this wall" was delivered with just the right level of anger, strength, and command in his voice.

The understanding of the encoded message is directly influenced by changes in the voice. The pitch of our voice rises with a question and descends with a declarative statement. When we hear someone whose voice rises in pitch at the end of what seems to be a statement, what has been referred to as "uptalking," we receive a mixed message. Are we supposed to respond? Was that really a question?

The sender of the message should also be sure they are encoding their message at an understandable level of vocabulary usage. When sending a message to a child we will use different language than when sending messages to adults. One of the authors once knew someone who was self-conscious about her lack of higher education so she decided to improve her vocabulary by learning one page of the dictionary every day and using the new vocabulary. She soon discovered that none of her friends or acquaintances could understand her. She realized that her vocabulary had grown to a level that was incomprehensible to most people and she ended her daily vocabulary exercise. The same thing happens in the workplace. Managers may have a working vocabulary that significantly exceeds that of their staff. Using a vocabulary that is matched to the receiver's level of understanding is essential if you are to be understood.

"To everything there is a season" is a well-known quote. In the context of communication this quote has a particular meaning. There is a time for slang and colloquialisms and there is a time for formal language. Many ethnic, racial or age groups have developed their own slang or their own meaning for words in certain contexts. When trying to communicate with others one must be conscientious about not falling into a habit of using such slang. A simple example of this phenomenon is how we refer to soft drinks. In some regions of the country they use the word pop. In others they refer to soda, which describes carbonated water in some regions. In the south, the home of Coca Cola, it is common to hear people refer to all soft drinks as Coke. A corollary to this phenomenon is the use of brand names instead of a product name. Some years ago it was common to see signs posted at photocopiers that reminded users that not all copiers were Xerox copiers and therefore they were not Xeroxing but were photocopying. This campaign by Xerox was intended to remind people that Xerox was a respected name in copiers and the one they were using may not be a Xerox and therefore Xerox should not have its good name associated with it. The list of similar examples extends to Kleenex, Chapstick, and the previously mentioned use of Coke.

CHOOSING THE BEST CHANNEL

Channels of communication are categorized by their richness. That richness is determined by how much of the whole communication process is present—verbal and non-verbal. Thus, as channel richness increases, the chance for successful communication will increase and the process is made easier. In this section channels of communication will be discussed in ascending order of richness.

The least rich channel typically seen in businesses is the posted bulletin or memo. By posting the bulletin the sender is anticipating that the intended receivers of the communication will see the bulletin and read it. It is easy to see how this channel is so poor. There is no way for the sender to know if the message was ever received except through direct inquiry of the intended audience. In other words, the feedback to the sender that the message was received is not working. Another weakness of this channel is its ability to convey the full content of the communication. There are no non-verbal cues present and the intended tone may be easily misconstrued. Someone reading the bulletin may not be fully aware of the contextual aspects and thus interpret the meaning differently.

Only slightly better than the posted bulletin or memo are letters and memos sent to identified individuals. While there is an increased probability, perhaps even a certainty, that the intended recipient received the communication, all of the concerns about the lack of non-verbal cues are still present. Letters and memos have a higher probability of being responded to because of their personal nature, resulting in their increased richness. Electronic mail (e-mail) is an improvement over memos and letters because of its instantaneous transmission. E-mail also has the ability to send an automatic reply confirming its receipt when opened by the recipient. E-mail users have also developed a lexicon of symbols to provide some non-verbal cues. These symbols, called emoticons, can be used to suggest the sender is intending the content to be funny, the sender's mood (happy, sad, etc.) and the tone. For example, sending e-mail in all capital letters is considered to be the equivalent of shouting. E-mail, because of its typical informality also makes use of abbreviations that would seem out of place in letters or memos. For instance LOL stands for laughing out loud and the letter U substitutes for the word you. As suggested by these examples, the use of abbreviations may provide some non-verbal cues and may be used as time saving devices.

Voice mail, if used effectively, is the next richest channel. What do we mean by effectively? If voice mail is used to communicate, and not just leave a message requesting a return call, it can expedite actions. Most people have experience the "phone tag" phenomenon in which two people repeatedly call each other and leave a message requesting a return call. This process can sometimes go on for days when all the initiator of the communication needed to do was indicate the reason for their call by giving some information or asking the question they want answered. The following exchange illustrates this point.

Caller: "Please call me back and let me know when the shipment to ABC Company will go out."

Recipient (in a return call): "The shipment to ABC Company went out this morning."

Those two telephone calls resulted in a question being asked and answered. Managers in particular should be conscientious in their use of voice mail to set the example for other staff. Since the voice provides non-verbal cues in its tone and inflection, this channel is a significant step forward. However, the inability to confirm receipt of the message immediately tempers the effectiveness of voice mail.

Speeches are a richer format than voice mail. The audience can see the non-verbal cues and the speaker can see the reactions of the audience. Obviously the speaker needs to be able to "read" the reactions of the audience to know if a statement was understood or not, or to gauge the level of attention being given the speech. What is missing from this channel is active interaction between the sender and the receiver of the message; the interaction is passive on the part of the audience. Therefore the feedback is limited to the speaker's ability to correctly interpret the listener's reaction.

Telephone conversations are a fairly rich channel for communication. Many non-verbal cues can be provided in the voice, the opportunity for immediate feedback and checking of understanding is present, and the process is fully interactive. However, telephone conversations are lacking an important ingredient. The lack of visual contact leaves a large portion of the non-verbal cues absent.

The richest communication channel is face-to-face. With modern technology that can mean teleconferencing. While teleconferencing is not true face-to-face communication, it is close enough that we will discuss them together. Face-to-face communication allows for the full communication to take place in real time with all non-verbal aspects of the communication also present. The sender has the full array of communication tools available, including body language, gestures and facial expressions. The receiver can provide instantaneous feedback to the sender and the sender can instantly confirm that the listener understood the message intended. Both parties also know the context, thus eliminating one possible source for misinterpretation of written communication. Videoconferencing may present some delays because of transmission delays, and sound quality can affect the clear understanding of vocal inflections and intonations and pronunciation. However, those aspects of videoconferencing present a minimal degrading of the communication process.

Clearly the choice of channel is dependent on availability, the situation, and the parties involved. Generally, the richest possible should always be chosen. When less rich channels are used, the sender and receiver must take on the additional challenges associated with the loss of some of the communication elements like nonverbal cues. The sender will have to carefully encode the message and the receiver will have to be sure to confirm correct understanding. Managers have to be particularly cognizant of channel limitations. When managers communicate with employees it is typically very important that the communication be clear and successful, or the employee will be left with a poorer understanding of what is expected, what the assignment was, or what actions they are to take. Managers can reduce this confusion by asking the employee to restate what the manager said. That means the sender (manager) must take on more responsibility for confirming the communication was successful. Do not ask "Do you understand?" ask the receiver to repeat back to you what you said.

RECEIVING COMMUNICATION FOR CLEAR UNDERSTANDING

Our experience has shown that most of us are not nearly as proficient at receiving information as we are at sending the message. This could be a result of being taught how to talk but not ever being taught how to listen. Our ability to receive written communication is, of course, directly correlated to our ability to read and comprehend. This section will focus primarily on listening since that is a skill not routinely taught in schools. The key to effective listening is to be active. Most people have probably observed that some people seem to have "natural" conversation skills while others seem to not be very good at conversing. The difference is often the listening skills of the individuals. Active listening can be learned through practice and will significantly improve the effectiveness of communication. There are six behaviors and actions that can greatly improve listening.

1. The most important step in active listening is not talking. It is impossible to listen and talk at the same time. The human brain will quickly become overwhelmed.
2. Pay attention. Focus on what the speaker is saying, not on what you are going to say in response. A good rule of thumb is to let one or two seconds pass before you respond. That will allow you time to formulate your response and confirm that the speaker is finished what they were saying. From our experience, that pause is typically the most difficult behavior change for most people.
3. Maintain appropriate eye contact. Maintaining eye contact let's the speaker know that you are paying attention. Be aware of the cultural norms for eye contact.
4. Use verbal and non-verbal cues to let the speaker know you are listening. Body language like nodding the head and verbal acknowledgements ("uh huh", "yes", "I see") let the speaker know you are listening. Posture can also let the speaker know you are listening. Leaning toward the speaker or sitting straight is better than slouching or reclining.
5. Check your understanding. Restate what you heard and check with the sender that your understanding is accurate. Do not just repeat the words used by the person speaking to you, but put your understanding into your own words.

6. Ask questions. Questions can be used to confirm your understanding—"Are you saying?" Questions can also be used to ask for clarification—"I don't understand, can you say that again?"

Regular practice of these behaviors will improve your ability to actively listen. Remembering that listening requires conscious action will become more automatic with ongoing practice of the active listening steps above. Being a better listener will make the manager's job easier since he or she will more clearly understand what is being said to them. That understanding will reduce conflicts caused by misunderstanding, will save time wasted doing something that was not necessary if they had understood what was said, and enable the manager to be more responsive/supportive to the employees.

NOISE AND BARRIERS

Noise in the context of the communication model above is anything that interferes with the process. That includes audible and visual stimuli that serve to distract the participants from giving full attention to the communication. Having a television on while carrying on a conversation, people moving about during a lecture, a door opening or closing, and a cell phone ringing or vibrating during conversation are all forms of noise. Barriers to communication are related to the personality and experiences of the individuals involved. Filtering is the process of manipulating the message so it will be favorably received. When an employee tells a manager what the manager wants to hear the employee is filtering the communication. Some of the recent accounting scandals would appear to present examples of filtering. Allegedly, shareholders were given information that indicated the companies' performance was better than the reality so the stock prices climbed.

Selective perception results when the receiver sees or hears the message based on their own needs, motivation, personal characteristics, and experiences. An employee who enters a performance appraisal expecting to hear bad news is likely to perceive the appraisal negatively even if that is not really the case. A closely related barrier to communication is projection. Projection is the process of projecting one's interests and expectations into the communication. For example, a manager who expects younger workers to be less capable may find more "problems" with a report than the same manager will find with a more mature worker, even if the reports are of equal quality.

Most of us have experienced information overload at some time. Information overload is a barrier to effective communication because we are receiving more information than we are able to process in a meaningful way. Consider how many communiqués the typical manager receives in a day— email, instant messaging, voice mail, telephone calls, written reports, verbal reports and requests—and it is easy to understand how information overload can occur. We have known managers who report receiving as many as fifty to seventy-five emails per day alone.

Emotions, gender differences, and cultural barriers all present potential barriers to communication. Our emotional state at the time of the communication must be considered. Someone who is angry will not receive a message the same as someone who is excited or happy to hear the information. There have been numerous books written about the differences in communication approaches between men and women. Two well-known examples are Deborah Tannen's *You Just Don't Understand* and John Gray's *Men Are From Mars, Women Are From Venus.* Cultural differences exist even within the same country. Anyone who has traveled to different regions of the United States can attest to cultural differences in communication. In the south it is quite common for people to refer to everyone as "dear" "honey" "darlin'" or some similar endearment. In some regions those terms would be cause for a claim of sexual harassment. Being aware of the possible sources of noise and the potential barriers to communication and striving to reduce them are important to effective communication.

TO DO LIST:

- Practice editing by reading some company publications and trying to make the writing more clear.
- Record (sound or video) yourself speaking to employees and review the recording. Pay particular attention to diction, tone, volume, inflections and clarity of the message.
- Make a list of the slang and colloquialisms you typically use and make a conscious effort to eliminate them one by one.
- Practice active listening by keeping the list of behaviors given above nearby and checking off those you did well and those you need to work on after every discussion you have with a subordinate.
- Evaluate the communication channels you have used in the past week and rank them for their potential effectiveness. Identify alternate channels that could have been more effective.
- Evaluate your work space and work environment for potential noise sources and try to eliminate as many as possible.
- Think about the possible influences your personal experiences, expectations, and personality may have on you sending and receiving communications and identify steps you can take to try to counteract those possible barriers.

Chapter 4
Leading Effective Employees

The first thing to understand about leadership is that there is no *one* way to effectively lead in the workplace. The history of management research reveals many efforts to find the most effective leadership approach for maximum performance. That century of research has made it clear that different situations call for different leadership styles or approaches. The focus of this chapter will be on the kinds of variables that may influence the effectiveness of different leadership approaches and suggestions from the research about what to do in those different situations. While it would be nice to identify specific action or steps to follow for effective leadership, that is not possible. However, a brief discussion of leadership behaviors, styles, and approaches is necessary. For the purposes of this chapter we will discuss leadership behaviors as the manifestation of different leadership approaches or styles.

LEADERSHIP BEHAVIORS

Leadership behaviors can be classified into two broad categories that were the focus of much of the management leadership research. One set of behaviors will be called task behaviors. The other set of behaviors will be called people behaviors.

Task behaviors are those that generally are targeted at the how and when of task completion. Task behaviors are leader behaviors such as giving instructions, pointing out deadlines, providing specific work schedules and assignments, achieving efficiency, and keeping costs low. As one can easily see, the attention in task behaviors is given to "getting the job done" in the most efficient and expeditious manner. These kinds of leader behaviors were the driving force behind the early success of the industrial revolutions when large-scale production and standardized products came into being.

Task behaviors are frequently seen in fast food restaurants. The very concept of fast food is that providing customers' meals quickly drives the service aspect of the business. The consistency of the product drives the product side of the business. What does one typically see during the lunch rush at atypical fast food restaurant? Employees have very specific tasks they are assigned. The manager is typically directing the workers by giving instructions.

The cooking staff is told what they need to be preparing to maintain the inventory. The cleaning/maintenance personnel are being instructed whether to attend to tables or floors or trash containers. The counter staff is being monitored to be sure customers are being served in a timely manner. And, the manager seems to be almost completely attending to efficiency.

Clearly, there is a need to pay attention to completing the tasks, but is that enough? Research tells us the answer to that question is no.

People behaviors are also necessary to maximize efficiency and effectiveness. People behaviors are those behaviors that demonstrate respect for subordinates' ideas and feelings, develop trust and teamwork, provide open communication, and are generally supportive of employees. Some may argue that these behaviors are not appropriate because the workplace should be a place where people focus on the work to be done. However, a significant body of management research has clearly demonstrated the value of these people behaviors. People behaviors are frequently seen in software development. It is quite common for very complex software programs to be developed by teams. These teams will typically gather together regularly to discuss the purpose of the software, develop an overall approach to the problem and then assign sections of the code to each employee to write. Because each project is unique and will require new ideas and approaches to create an effective end product, the personnel writing the code have to have open communication, respect for the work of the others in the team, and be open to suggestions and ideas of team members about how to solve the problem. This kind of project is not likely to succeed if each team member just does exactly what he or she is told in the specific manner they are told to do it. Clearly in this situation the leader should be using people behaviors to create trust, teamwork, respect and open communications, not giving instructions about what, how, and when to do specific tasks.

The challenge for leaders in the work place is to exhibit the most effective behaviors for the specific situation they face. The difficulty with this seemingly simple notion is that it requires the leader to be able to assess the situation accurately. In other words, effective management leadership requires one to be able to accurately evaluate a situation and act on that situation with effective leader behaviors. To further complicate this challenge, one must recognize that no two situations are going to be exactly alike, even if they appear to be the same. Situations in the workplace, while they may appear similar, are typically influenced by human characteristics that will not be the same. It is these human characteristics that are often the one variable that is different between two seemingly similar situations.

CONTINGENCY LEADERSHIP VARIABLES

There are several theories that suggest different variables that influence the effectiveness of different leadership behaviors. All of those theories have been shown to have some validity through research. For our purposes the situational variables from those different theories will be considered together since no single set of variable has been shown to be complete. The variables can be broadly categorized into two groups—situational and human. The situational variables relate to the work environment, organization variables, and the kind of tasks. The human variables relate to the employees' skills, abilities, and motivation.

Situational Variables

Work situations contain many possible variables that could influence the effectiveness of leader behaviors. The kind of task is one such variable. In the examples of the fast food restaurant and the software development firm given earlier it should be apparent that the tasks involved have very different characteristics. The fast food chain has tasks that are structured since they can be clearly defined in terms of specific, often repetitive, actions to take to complete the tasks. The software development challenge is quite different. Every program is going to be different and therefore must be approached as a brand new task. It is impossible to establish a set of specific actions that can be done the same way every time to bring about computer programs that are each unique. The software development process is one with unstructured tasks; each time the job is done it may be different from the previous time. As shown in the examples of task behaviors in the examples above, it is obvious that the degree of task specialization is an important variable to consider when deciding on the best leader behavior. The more specialized the task the more precise instructions and training are typically used to be sure employees are performing the task "correctly" every time, but once the task is learned the leader can focus on people behaviors. With less specialized tasks one usually will be more task focused because the tasks will not be repeatedly the same and thus the people performing them will need more guidance. However, as we will see later, these generalizations must take into account additional variables, particularly the human variables. In other words, the leader cannot focus on only one variable to determine the best approach for a given situation.

Another work situation variable to consider is the source and strength of power of the leader. Is the leader in a position that carries with it certain inherent powers such as hiring and firing? Are the leader's decisions strongly supported by higher management, or often overruled? Is the leader using his or her knowledge or expertise as the basis for their power? Do the subordinates respect that expertise and freely acknowledge it, thereby giving it more strength, or are they suspicious of it, thus weakening its influence? Leaders who have the respect of the followers are not likely to need to use task behaviors as much. Subordinates will meet deadlines and generally do a good job because they acknowledge the leader's expertise and respect his or her power. On the other hand, leaders who exercise a lot of power based on their position may, or may not, have the same level of respect and may have to exhibit more task behaviors to get the same level of performance.

As just alluded to, the basis and strength of the power the leader possesses must also take into consideration the relationship between the leader and the subordinates. A leader operating from a position of power may be able to focus on people behaviors if that leader has good working relationships with the subordinates. That respect could result from the subordinates' recognition that the leader was deserving of the position because of his or her knowledge or skills. The respect could also result from the subordinates recognizing that the leader is fair or has personal attributes that warrant their respect.

Human Variables

The human variables of primary interest are the employee's willingness or enthusiasm for the work and the employee's ability to do the work. Clearly an employee who has been successfully doing a job for some years is likely to be more skilled than a newly hired individual. The experienced employee will likely need less instruction and specific guidance than the new employee. For the newly hired employees more task focused behaviors will be necessary in the beginning while the more experienced and skilled employees will be best served by the leader focusing on people behaviors. The new employee may be a college graduate who has the essential knowledge for the job but will most often still need specific training and guidance to learn the organization's way of doing things. Employees who are enthusiastic and willing to perform at high levels of productivity are likely to need less direct supervision or monitoring of their actions and will very possibly be more quickly trained. In that instance the amount of task focused behaviors by the leader will be lower than for the unenthusiastic employee.

An example case will illustrate the impact of human variables. One of the authors was the director of a department with approximately twenty-five employees. Three of those employees were supervisors. One of the supervisors had been promoted by a previous director because of his excellent knowledge of the department's tasks and his reliable performance. This employee would seem to be one for who people focused behaviors would be appropriate since he was highly knowledgeable and competent. However, that leadership approach was not successful. The employee continued to perform his supervisory duties in a minimally satisfactory manner, but in no way did he demonstrate the excellence that led to the initial promotion to a supervisory position. A closer evaluation of the situation clarified this change in performance. While the employee was successful in a front line staff position where he was highly skilled, he was not interested in moving into higher management. Since he was not enthusiastic about moving to higher level management, he was not willing to perform at the high level necessary for further promotion. Further evaluation revealed that he also only had minimal supervisory skills. Thus, the assessment revealed that he was not very skilled at the new position nor enthusiastic about developing the necessary skills. Therefore, a focus on task behaviors by the leader would be more appropriate, especially since the task was also unstructured and not repetitive. This supervisor needed to be told specifically what to do, when to do it, and how to do it. Clearly the focus on the human variable was a problem in this case because of the combination of human and situational variables.

APPLYING SITUATIONAL LEADERSHIP

Successful leadership in the workplace today requires the effective application of the principles of situational leadership. Leaders need to assess the situation in terms of the task being done, the skills and enthusiasm of the employees doing the tasks, the nature of the relationship between the leader and the followers, and the source and strength of the leader's power. The remainder of this chapter will present examples of different combinations of the variables and why certain leadership approaches would be appropriate.

An employee is performing a relatively structured task that consists of specific steps to be performed in a specific sequence. That employee has worked at the job for several years and is required to regularly review the procedures, so they should be very capable of doing the job accurately and efficiently. The leader has the power to discipline the employee but the rewards the leader can offer are generally non-tangible. All disciplinary actions are subject to review by the leader's supervisor. The leader has not taken any significant disciplinary actions related to job performance. The employee respects the leader and recognizes the leader is highly skilled and knowledgeable about the job. The tangible rewards the employee will receive for doing an excellent job are an annual cost of living salary adjustment that will be the same for all employees, and the availability of overtime that is typically assigned on a seniority basis.

An analysis of the situation above should reveal the following situational characteristics. The task is structured. The relationship between the leader and follower appears to be somewhat positive. The employee seems to be highly qualified but may be only marginally enthusiastic or willing to perform at a high level of efficiency with no tangible incentives for excellent performance. The willingness of higher management to support the leader's actions is unknown since there have not been any occasions to determine the strength of that support. What kind of leadership behaviors should one use in this situation? It appears from the facts available that a balance of task and people behaviors may be called for. Rely on the good relationship to allow for more task focus, provide clear, specific instructions for the tasks while allowing the employee to suggest ways to improve the current methods based on his or her experience. Make the rewards and consequences resulting from performance very specific. The next chapter will provide guidance on using positive feedback to increase employee satisfaction.

Another situation is quite different. A highly qualified and enthusiastic individual with a graduate degree is newly hired into a position that is very unstructured. In fact, every workday presents new situations that call for using differing approaches or skills to complete the task. The organization is new and still establishing procedures and operational protocols. The leader is highly skilled, personable, patient and very well respected by the followers. Since this is a new organization, the leader is the most senior person in the hierarchy. An assessment of this situation suggests a people focused leadership approach. Why? The follower is highly skilled and very willing, the leader is operating from a firm base of power that leaves no question about whether higher management will support his or her actions, and the leader is highly respected by the followers. However, the tasks are very unstructured and might suggest a need to be more task focused. But, the follower is highly skilled and procedures and protocols are in the development stage. A people focused leader in this instance will be able to involve the followers in developing the procedures and therefore build a sense of ownership of the procedures among the followers. This can be done by building trust, involving the employee in decisions by working as a team, establishing open communications, and allowing the employee to make mistakes that are then used as learning opportunities.

The two examples discussed above point out the challenge of situational leadership. Any situation is likely to present conflicting components during the assessment and require the leader to make judgements about the relative importance of each variable. This potential conflict is the essence of the challenge to effective leaders. The leader's ability to analyze the situation accurately is a skill that is gained primarily through trial and error. In the example of the department director discussed previously, the leader struggled for some time to identify why their efforts to improve the performance of the supervisor in question were fruitless. It was only after recognizing that the individual in question was not interested in career advancement that the director could understand that a more task oriented approach was called for. In management education there is a widespread acceptance that management is part science and part art. Being successful at the art of accurately "reading" a situation is often what separates excellent leaders and managers from the pack.

TO DO LIST

- Evaluate the job tasks of the people you lead in terms of the degree of specialization and give them a score from one (very unspecialized) to ten (very specialized).
- Assess the skill level of each of the staff you lead and rate them on a five-point scale.
- Assess the enthusiasm, self-direction, and willingness of each of your staff on a five-point scale.
- Identify five specific task focused behaviors you can use that will be consistent with policies and practices in your organization.
- Identify five specific people focused behaviors you can apply in your organization.

- Using a ten-point scale identify the level of support you would expect to receive from your supervisor for the decisions you make, especially those related to the behaviors in the previous lists.
- Identify the best balance of task and people focus for each of your staff based on the assessments above.
- Develop an action plan to use the behaviors identified as appropriate and evaluate their effectiveness.

Chapter 5
Motivating People by Meeting Their Needs

To be successful motivating employees managers need to understand the origin of motivation. It is common practice to talk about motivating employees. However, we present the discussion of motivation from a slightly different perspective that some might argue is semantic, but brings about a change in how managers approach the process. It can be argued that managers do not motivate employees. Employees have an inherent motivation that the manager needs to trigger or activate. If we start with the premise that people are inherently motivated, the role of the manager becomes one of discovering what will activate that process. That approach also requires us to recognize that different employees will have differing levels of motivation and some employees will be more easily encouraged than others will. This perspective on motivation also suggests that individuals' motivation is stimulated by differing management actions. The challenges for managers then become discovering the catalysts for each employee, identification of ways to introduce the catalyst, and carefully targeted implementation of the actions needed. This chapter will address each of those challenges individually and illustrate how they are interdependent.

CATALYSTS FOR MOTIVATION

The management research literature on the subject of what motivates employees is quite voluminous. Much of that research focuses on the idea that people are motivated to satisfy some need or want. That is to say, we strive to acquire something we deem to be important to our ongoing survival, happiness, self-esteem, or sense of well being. There have been numerous theories proposed to identify the needs we try to fulfill just as there have been studies about the relative importance of different means of satisfying needs. Interestingly, in studies asking employees what they want most from their job and then asking managers what employees want most from their jobs the results have been consistent over the years. Managers consistently rank salary or pay at, or very near, the top of the list while employees rank salary or pay typically in the middle of the list. This kind of discrepancy clearly points to the need for managers to really understand what employees are seeking in their work. While salary and pay typically are ranked in the middle of a list of needs that does not mean people are not motivated by money. It just means that there is variety in the needs of a group of employees.

So, what do people want from their jobs? Obviously the answer to that question depends on the individual. We do know from research that we can broadly categorize employee needs. There are several models that classify needs into different schemas. For our purposes we have synthesized those models into three kinds of needs—security, relationship, and personal growth.

Security

For people who are trying to establish a level of basic financial and personal security, their needs include things like a wage that enables them to provide essential necessities such as food and shelter, a safe work and living environment, and a sense of security in those areas. For individuals with security needs the employer must think about ways to increase their sense of security. That sense of security can be enhanced in a number of ways. The most obvious thing to do is ensure that the wages you are paying are competitive and fair for the market in which you operate. If your wage scale is not competitive, employees will feel undervalued. That is not to say that competitive pay is sufficient; it is necessary. However, there are many other considerations to increase employees' sense of well being. Working conditions that are safe, comfortable, properly equipped, and respectful will help increase employee feelings of security. Do the facilities need to be painted or refurbished? Do employees have the necessary equipment to do their jobs? Is the equipment well maintained and in good working condition? Does the climate control system work properly in all work areas? Is the equipment, including things like chairs and desks, comfortable or does it create physical and/or emotional stress? Is the work environment respectful of individual differences in a way that everyone feels comfortable that they will not be subjected to unwanted, hostile, or inappropriate comments or actions from others? The answers to these questions will provide much needed information for managerial decisions about needed actions to improve employee working conditions.

A few specific examples will illustrate these issues. In a previous management position one of the authors had an administrative assistant whom developed a pinched nerve in her shoulders. After consulting with a physician it was discovered that the cause of the problem was the positioning of her computer and the equipment she used to hold the copy she was typing. A simple attachment that cost less than twenty dollars solved the problem and prevented further injury and lost work time. Simply analyzing the workstation of employees for ergonomic comfort can provide increased job satisfaction. Employees who use computers for their work are prone to eyestrain or carpal tunnel problems. Providing screen filters and wrist pads are simple solutions to make the work environment more satisfactory. We regularly hear workers describe offices that are too cold or too hot for comfort because windows are not properly sealed and allow drafts or are exposed to too much afternoon sun and do not have adequate ways to block the sun. To have dissatisfied employees because of something as simple and inexpensive as blinds is fiscally illogical. Spending a small amount of resources (time and/or financial) can lead to significant reductions in costly turnover and lost productivity.

Job security is also a very significant way to increase motivation. The sense of well being provided by not having to worry about being laid off is quite important to motivation. Employees who feel no commitment from their employer are not going to reciprocate with loyalty of their own. If employees are worrying about their job security they are likely to be less motivated to excel because they see no benefit to such behavior if they are going to be "let go" at the first signs of trouble Employees that perceive the employer as committed to finding ways to keep people employed realize significant benefits. Airtran Airways is an excellent example of this kind of commitment. After the September 11, 2001 terrorist attacks the airline industry suffered a tremendous blow. Airline reservations and travel dropped precipitously and caused large-scale layoffs in many airlines. Airtran took a different approach. The senior management explained the need for cuts in expenses to see the company through the crisis. They offered the employees the opportunity to save everyone's job if they all agreed to pay reductions, including senior management, or have a significant number of employees laid-off. The company promised to make the employees "whole" in terms of salary by means of bonuses when the airline returned to normal operations. The employees opted for the pay cuts with job security and Airtran continued to operate with all of its employees. Airtran was one of the first airlines to return to profitability while the major airlines continued to report record losses. The massive lay-offs by competitors also contributed to bad feelings and labor problems for several of those airlines. Lincoln Electric has operated with a guaranteed employment policy since its creation over sixty years ago. When faced with financial downturns or economic challenges, Lincoln has also asked employees to take reduced hours to protect everyone's job. While guaranteed employment is not feasible in all organizations, it is clear that job security can greatly increase motivation and performance.

Another catalyst for motivation is good management and supervision. Supervisors who are well trained, knowledgeable, and have good interpersonal skills improve the work environment. Supervisors need communication skills that equip them for giving instructions, feedback, and guidance in constructive ways that contribute to a good work environment. Supervisors who shout at employees, cannot control their temper, are unreasonable in their expectations, unfair in their treatment of subordinates, or generally do not create a positive work atmosphere free of fear, intimidation, and arbitrary or inconsistent actions and decisions are going to negatively impact the sense of security, and thus be less effective. Employees with supervisors who are fair, give constructive criticism in a positive manner, control their temper to avoid outbursts and shouting, provide positive feedback as much as constructive criticism, can provide clear guidance and instructions, are consistent in their application of policies, and try to create a congenial work environment will have more highly motivated employees.

Policies and procedures are another important aspect of working conditions since they help define the organization's culture. Employees who perceive policies and procedures as onerous, too inflexible, ambiguous or unclear, unfairly or unevenly applied, or unreasonable will not be satisfied with their jobs. Dissatisfied employees will be motivated to find other employment, not motivated to perform at high levels for the current employer.

Relationships

Many employees feel the security discussed above and need other outcomes from their work. Some employees value the personal interactions and the professional relationships that derive from their work. This relationship need may be satisfied in many ways. The current trend to more team based work is an excellent way to satisfy the need for relationships and interaction. Teams provide the opportunity to exchange ideas and learn from others' perspectives. Teams also require interaction with other people. There have been cases of employees whose performance deteriorates because the work environment was changed and employees no longer interacted with each other but worked individually.

If a team approach is not feasible for the type of work one can consider other means to bring people together in the work setting. Assigning two or more people to work on a special project will allow for interactions. On the job training is an excellent way to allow interaction between workers. Assigning new hires to observe and learn from experienced employees will allow both employees to satisfy a need for relationships and interaction.

The relationship need can be met in other ways not specifically linked to the work people do. Employees may satisfy this need by interacting with coworkers in a common lunch or break area. For this to be effective employees need to feel free to take breaks and lunch periods away from their workstation. Employees can be encouraged to take their lunch periods rather than "working through lunch" or taking lunch breaks at their desk or workstation. These measures can be achieved with no cost to the organization. Other mechanisms for providing the chance for human interaction include company recreational activities. Many companies have softball teams or participate in bowling leagues. These activities bring employees together in a fun environment that allows relationships to be built. When the employees return to work after such activities they feel more a part of the organization and have a sense of being part of the group, even if their work is performed individually.

Team building exercises can also facilitate a sense of being part of a group and thus help satisfy the need for relationships. While a full discussion of team building is not within the scope of this book, there are many sources available for guidance in this area.

Personal Growth

Personal growth is frequently listed by employees as the most important motivator, far more so than money. To address this challenge we must first establish a meaning for the phrase. In this context personal growth refers to learning, having more responsibility, and the opportunity to advance. In other words, personal growth needs are related to professional development. From our experience as managers these needs, while often the strongest from the employee perspective, are typically the least recognized or addressed by managers. The arguments we have heard from managers for this phenomenon are quite varied. The arguments range from concern about the costs of professional development and training to concern about assigning work to individuals that is not in their job description to the legality of asking an employee to perform a "higher level" task without adjusting their pay. These are all legitimate concerns to a point. However, there are many things managers can do to provide opportunities for personal growth. One thing that can be done is to have clearly defined career tracks with well defined job descriptions that specify the skills, knowledge and abilities expected of someone in that job. This approach will make it clear what one needs in order to be prepared for promotions. Some companies are now defining career tracks for management and professional staff. Professional career tracks allow the opportunity for growth in income and responsibility without having to assume a management position for which an employee may not have the skills. For example, a career track for engineers could be developed by establishing levels of engineering competency needed before one is assigned to different levels of projects. An entry engineer may be assigned to basic projects with more experienced staff while more advanced engineers with more experience, training, and education may be assigned to work on complex projects independently.

Special assignments are an outstanding way to fulfill a need for personal growth. A temporary assignment to work on a project that furthers one's knowledge, skills, or abilities will enhance that employee's value to the company and give the employee some experience that will help prepare them for higher positions. For example, a manager who has to prepare a budget can ask an employee who has management potential to help prepare the budget. This becomes a learning opportunity for the employee and also demonstrates that the manager has confidence and respect for the employee's abilities. Demonstrating such confidence also serves to enhance the employee's self confidence which is, in itself, a way to facilitate personal growth. A word of caution is required here. Offering opportunities to take on special assignments must be made with a genuine desire to help the personal development of the employee and not as a way to "dump" the assignment on a subordinate. The perception that the assignment is being dumped on a subordinate will have the opposite effect of what was intended. It is important that the discussion of the potential assignment be sincerely presented as an opportunity to learn new skills, develop one's abilities and skills further, and/or as a step to further responsibilities and eventual promotion.

Interestingly, sometimes the simple actions of managers are the most effective. Employees' needs for personal growth may be partly fulfilled by simple recognition of their accomplishments. When employees accomplish tasks or assignments in a timely, efficient, or effective manner, recognize that accomplishment and acknowledge it. Personal growth for some employees will mean they have mastered their job, an assignment, or a task. For others, the need to do an excellent job is a manifestation of their need for personal growth. When an employee completes a particularly difficult task, meets a tight deadline, helps satisfy a disgruntled customer, or in any other way helps the organization achieve its goals, that behavior should be recognized and acknowledged. That recognition need not necessarily be more than a simple statement of appreciation in many cases. The absence of such simple recognition can, and likely will, become a source of job dissatisfaction. Dissatisfied employees are motivated most to find a more satisfying job. We have frequently asked workers how often their boss acknowledges a job well done. Typically the answer is never or very infrequently. When we turn that around and ask how often mistakes are recognized and result in some consequence the answer typically is always. When we have asked workers what would help the most to motivate them to do a good job, the answer typically is recognition and thanks. If you want your employees to be motivated to keep performing at high levels, let them know you see what they are doing and appreciate it. That will help them realize a sense of accomplishment, which goes directly to their desire for personal growth and development.

Highly satisfied and motivated employees are highly productive and less likely to leave their jobs. That means a significant reduction in turnover, which means significant savings from the cost of turnover. As a manager, would you rather spend money on a sure positive return or spend it on a potential positive return? Many times when a skilled employee leaves for lack of personal growth or development opportunities you have to spend money to hire and train an unknown person who may never be as productive as the one who left. Chances are you will also have to pay them more because the market has outpaced your organization's and employee's annual salary growth. It is a fairly common expression that you have to change jobs to keep up with the market as far as salary. So, how can you reduce the likelihood of employees leaving? Besides doing the things already discussed, provide training and professional development opportunities. One of the authors is a good example of this concept. When employed early in his career he was given promotions and plenty of recognition. However, his growth potential was limited by his education. The employer, through an educational assistance plan helped him complete his degree by reimbursing some of the tuition costs. This practice is common for employees seeking MBAs. Often the assistance comes with a requirement of a commitment to continue to work for the employer providing the assistance.

There are less expensive means to provide professional growth opportunities. Training offered by the employer, even if outside trainers are paid to provide the training, should realize positive returns on the investment. More highly educated and well-trained employees are more productive, more effective, and better prepared to contribute positively to the bottom line. Employer provided training also allows for economies of scale since many employees will be trained at once; thus, making the per capita cost lower.

The Process of Motivation

One of the most straightforward ways of think about the process of motivation is to think of the end and then derive a means. The end is the satisfaction of a need with an outcome that has value. In order to achieve that end the employee must perform at a commensurate level. The employee will perform at the level if the outcome is of sufficient value. The manager's role is to ensure that the outcome will result and provide the necessary resources for the task to be completed. These resources can be training as discussed in an earlier chapter, equipment and physical resources as highlighted here, and organizational resources such as effective leadership, feedback, and communication which will be discussed in later chapters.

INTERDEPENDENCE OF MOTIVATION APPROACHES

While the discussion thus far may seem to imply that each employee will be motivated if the manager focuses on the one central need, which could not be farther from the truth. The levels of need—security, relationship, and personal growth—are interdependent. Nor do they typically manifest themselves one at a time. All the levels of need are likely to be present in each employee. The challenge for the manager is to comprehend the interdependent nature of these needs. The relative prominence of the needs will vary according to the situation the employee faces at any given time. For example, an employee who is trying to pay off student loans or establish some financial security to buy a house may today be focused on security needs primarily. That does not mean those employees do not have relationship and personal growth needs that also need the manager's attention. Those employees may be primarily concerned with job security and income but their long term commitment and satisfaction will require that other needs be met as well. Managers must develop the ability to anticipate the time when the employees' focus will change or adjust. The manager needs to be able to anticipate the subtle shifts in focus and understand their impact on motivation.

This last point can be highlighted by an example. Suppose the manager has a number of employees who are experienced and highly skilled. The manager is likely trying to provide growth opportunities for these employees since that is what the manager expects them to be concerned with. However, the manager does not recognize that two of the employees in his or her department are in their late fifties. The manager also does not know that one of those employees is dealing with an aging parent who has been declining in health. It is very reasonable for the manager to conclude that both employees are likely to be interested in the opportunity for personal growth at this stage in their successful careers. However, there may be an even more pressing need. These employees are approaching retirement and one is facing the possibility of having to care for and provide more assistance (financial and personal) to an aging parent. The impending retirements may lead the employees to be concerned about their financial security and thus lead them to be concerned with making as much money as possible to be able save it to live on when they retire. One of these employees may also need a more flexible work schedule to be able to attend to the parent's needs. If the manager only sees the need for personal growth and does not recognize that other needs are also present, he or she could be frustrated to find that the employees are not as motivated as before, or that these highly skilled and experienced employees leave the company for better pay and flexible work schedules.

The challenge for managers is to develop the skill to detect changes in employees' priorities and make adjustments as needed. The difficulty in this "simple" solution is that such skills are very hard to develop and virtually impossible to teach. The ability to correctly identify employee need is developed through experience and by developing a working environment of trust and openness. Trusting and open environments facilitate relationship development. Managers who develop solid positive relationships with their subordinates are more likely to be successful at identifying employee needs and recognizing subtle shifts in those needs.

TO DO LIST

- Meet with each of your employees individually and ask what they want most from their jobs.
- Make a list of at least five specific actions you can take to increase employees' sense of security, and then implement those things.
- Walk through your work area and evaluate it in terms of its design and comfort level. Is the environment clean, safe, and appropriately warm or cool? Do people seem to be working in awkward or uncomfortable positions? Hint: Ask them.
- Make sure the employees have the resources they need—equipment, supplies, etc. Again, ask them.
- Evaluate the work processes to insure they do not isolate people unnecessarily.
- Watch how employees interact with co-workers. Are their interactions constructive and positive or argumentative and divisive?
- Identify and implement five ways you can provide personal growth opportunities for your employees.
- Ask your employees what resources they need to increase the probability of successfully completing their assigned work.

- In conjunction with those employees, develop a plan to put any needed resources in place.

Chapter 6
Reinforcing Behavior and Providing Feedback

It is a phenomenon we are all familiar with. You have been doing your job the way you think it should be done but you wonder: "is my boss satisfied with my performance? He or she has not told me there is a problem but they have not told me my work is satisfactory either." Employees need to know how they are doing. Effective feedback does not only include pointing out mistakes or errors; it also includes regularly letting staff know when they are performing well. This chapter will discuss what managers should do to be sure their employees have an accurate picture of their performance. We will discuss establishing performance standards in Chapter 7. The focus of this chapter is the process of keeping staff informed about how you perceive their performance compared to the standards and using reinforcement to change and/or maintain acceptable behaviors and performance.

POSITIVE FEEDBACK

Beginning the discussion of feedback with positive feedback is not a random choice. Through our many years of teaching, management, and human resources experience the authors have learned that the lack of positive feedback is often a significant element in employee discontent. Repeatedly, if we ask students with part-time jobs, professionals, or any other full-time workers whether they think they receive enough feedback they respond with a resounding "no" or "only when I make a mistake" or some variation on the latter. It is pretty obvious that today's managers are not doing even a minimally adequate job of providing positive feedback.

What is positive feedback? Positive feedback is any feedback that, acknowledges, recognizes, or compliments when employees do their job. Notice that there was no qualifying adjective attached to the word job. Again, that is not by accident. The goal of managers is to have employees who perform their job at a high level of efficiency and effectiveness. That does not, however, mean that only excellence should be acknowledged or recognized by the manager. Employees will find it very difficult to become excellent if they do not even know if they are doing the job that is expected of them. If the manager never informs the employee that he or she is performing the tasks of the job in an acceptable manner, the employee has no way of knowing. If employees know they are doing the job correctly, they can attend to improving their performance.

Specific Types of Positive Feedback

Positive feedback comes in the form of acknowledgement, recognition, or compliments. Each of these will be considered separately. Acknowledgement is the most basic form of positive feedback. Acknowledgements can be verbal or written, private or public. Probably the simplest acknowledgement is a basic courtesy: saying thanks when the employee does something asked of them. Another simple means of acknowledgement is to tell employees that you know they are putting forth a good effort or they are getting the job done. This acknowledgement is often in the form of a verbal statement that indicates the manager is aware of the employees' performance. As indicated previously, these acknowledgements can be done in private or publicly. Managers should be sensitive to the individual employee and his or her comfort level with public acknowledgements. Examples of the effectiveness of acknowledging employee performance are easy to find. Ask co-workers to identify a time when they received a thank you for putting special effort into an assignment. Then ask them if they would be inclined to make a similar effort in the future. Our experience with that simple exercise consistently illustrates that employees will be willing to put forth similar effort again with the minimal expectation that their efforts will be acknowledged.

Recognition as positive feedback takes the concept of acknowledgement to the next level. Instead of simply acknowledging that a job is being done, recognition contains an element of quality. Recognition frequently involves a more formal process. The simplest form of recognition is a verbal statement that acknowledges the quality of the performance—good, excellent, commendable, etc. More formal forms of recognition are commonly adopted in today's organization. One can regularly see public displays in businesses recognizing "employees of the month" or letters sent by customers recognizing the work of specific employees. Many companies also have ceremonies to recognize outstanding performance as well as length of service. In the real estate industry it is common practice to run advertisements in local newspapers to recognize sales associates for achieving different sales levels. Typically these advertisements show photos of the individual sales agents arranged by level of sales. Anyone who has worked with a real estate agent also knows that it is common practice for their business cards to indicate that they have achieved a specific sales level such as the million-dollar club. Interestingly, in many cities one would only have to sell four or five houses per year to reach one million in sales. Selling a house every three months may not sound like a very successful agent but they still receive the recognition to encourage their future performance.

Compliments are closely related to recognition but go to the next level of positive feedback because they always have a positive value added. Compliments are a positive expression of the manager's satisfaction with employees' performance. Compliments will contain positive adjectives as qualifiers—good, excellent, admirable, nice, superior, etc. Compliments, because of the qualifiers, typically have a greater effect than recognition. Our experience as managers repeatedly illustrated this point. Compliments provide the additional benefit of specificity. Whereas employees often receive recognition for doing a good job over some time period, compliments recognize specific actions or completion of specific tasks. The effect of this specificity is to increase the feedback's impact on future performance. An example should clarify this point. On a recent airline flight one of the authors experienced a rather significant delay caused be engine problems that required diverting to an unintended destination. Flight crews in today's airlines are often over worked or have to cope with impatient, rude, or obnoxious passengers. On the flight mentioned the crew exhibited such professionalism under stress that several passengers readily complimented them when departing at the first stop on the flight that ultimately was delayed over six hours. This same crew continued to show the same professionalism until the end of the flight, even though they were, by then, at the end of a sixteen-hour day. The direct link of the compliments received to the specific actions on that flight was very effective for encouraging the crew to continue the excellent service. Would a general recognition of good performance have the same effect in such trying circumstances? Perhaps, but everyone has probably experienced a time when similar circumstances led to less then exemplary performance and customer service. Does that mean those personnel never received general recognition for doing their jobs well? That seems highly unlikely.

NEGATIVE FEEDBACK

Everyone we know has received negative feedback at some time in their career. For our purposes negative feedback is any actions or statements of management that criticize, find fault with, or point out mistakes in employee actions or behaviors. In fact, most of us have probably experienced or heard about instances of negative feedback much more than positive feedback. As noted before, when asked if they ever receive any negative feedback from their bosses, students and full-time employees will answer with a resounding yes, frequently supplemented with "all the time," or a similar sentiment. When asked if they receive regular positive feedback the same workers and students will say no. Does that mean negative feedback is bad? No. Negative feedback is an essential element of the manager's performance management efforts. The previous discussion is presented to make the point that negative feedback is, at least in the perception of the workers, used too often to be recognized as balanced with positive feedback.

Most management educators and trainers agree on several principles for negative feedback.

1. Negative feedback should be given in private if at all possible. Obviously if someone is doing something that is about to do harm to a person or otherwise have disastrous consequences managers cannot wait to correct the actions. However, barring an eminent disaster or harm a time should be set aside to talk about performance in private.

2. Negative feedback should have the goal of improving behaviors and correcting actions, not punishing. Feedback that identifies specific actions or behaviors and describes what should be done will be instructive while providing the opportunity to talk about how the employee's actions or behaviors differ from what is desired.

3. Negative feedback should be balanced with positive feedback.

4. Negative feedback should not be given in anger. Anger inhibits our ability to be logical, rational people. If negative feedback is going to be constructive and instructive it must be rational and logical.

5. Negative feedback is not likely to correct behaviors or actions by itself. It is only one of the many actions managers must take to maximize performance.

6. Negative feedback has the risk of accomplishing the opposite of what was intended. Employees who feel their performance is only criticized will have lower morale and job satisfaction. Morale and job satisfaction are two factors that will influence performance.

An example of using negative feedback to improve performance may help clarify this point. An employee has developed a pattern of missing work and not notifying the employer: in other words he is absent without leave. In a conference with him the manager informed the employee that it is unacceptable for him to not show up for work unless the absence is approved and he would be suspended for three days. However, the manager did not end the discussion at that point. The manager then continued the discussion by reminding the employee of the correct procedures for asking for and receiving time off. While this conversation may seem obvious and ridiculous to most of us, it is important to remember that many of our staff may have very different experiences than our own and may have acted the same way in a previous job with no consequences. Feedback is critical to reinforcing behaviors. The next section will discuss reinforcement and its uses to change behavior.

REINFORCEMENT

Reinforcement theory argues that actions or behaviors that are reinforced are more likely to occur again. Likewise, actions and behaviors that are ignored or punished will eventually decline and disappear. So, the challenge to managers is learning what reinforcement is, how to use it and when, while not attending to unwanted behaviors or actions. The first thing managers have to recognize is that their actions may be perceived quite differently than expected. A good example of this is attempts to punish. While the manager may be thinking he or she is punishing an employee by, for instance, sending them home for the rest of the day, the employee received just what he wanted because he really wanted to attend opening day at the baseball stadium. The reward of being able to attend opening day outweighed the "punishment" of being sent home for the day and losing several hours of pay. What is that employee likely to do the next time they want to attend an afternoon ball game? Whatever actions resulted in their being sent home the first time is what can be expected because the employee knows that behavior will result in "punishment." It cannot be overstated how important it is to know how the staff will perceive the consequences of their behaviors. It is absolutely critical to understand what the employee considers a reward. As discussed in Chapter Three, employees want different things. An effective reward for one person might be completely ineffective for another, and, as noted above, the manager's actions could be construed very differently than intended if the employee's needs are not taken into consideration.

Reinforcement comes in two forms. Positive reinforcement is the delivery of some positive reward when the desired actions or behaviors are exhibited. For example, an employee masters a new task during training and the trainer congratulates the employee, or an employee discovers a new way to do the job that is more efficient and receives a bonus. In both of these cases the reward resulted from the actions of the employee. It is critical that the link between the actions and the reward be clear and direct because whatever behavior or action was present immediately before the reward is received is the one that will be reinforced. Positive reinforcement should be delivered immediately after the desired behavior or action to eliminate the possibility of it being associated with another behavior. If that is not possible the connection between the reward and the action must be made very clear. We will discuss the amount and frequency of reinforcement to use later in this chapter.

Negative reinforcement is, for most people, a much more difficult approach to understand and use. In fact, the term negative reinforcement is frequently used incorrectly to suggest punishment. One way to think of negative reinforcement is in mathematical terms. The symbol for negative and subtraction are the same in mathematics. Therefore, negative reinforcement can be thought of as subtracting something. Since the goal of reinforcement is to increase good actions, the logic then follows that we should subtract something aversive that exists as the positive actions occur. For example, a new employee is being trained to operate a piece of equipment. The trainer is watching very closely and instructing in every step of the procedure, even though the employee is able to do the task completely on her own. The close oversight of the trainer is annoying to the employee because she feels she is not being trusted to do the task correctly. The trainer can reinforce the actions of the employee by subtracting the close scrutiny, which the employee dislikes. The trainer now lets the employee do the task on her own. The removal of the undesired scrutiny leads to the employee doing the task correctly repeatedly to avoid further close scrutiny.

Timing Reinforcement

The schedule of reinforcement is an important ingredient to its effectiveness. In the early stages of the process the reinforcement should occur very frequently. As the behaviors become more consistent, the reinforcement can be reduced. For example, if you are attempting to train an employee to perform a new task, each successive step that is performed correctly should be reinforced. This will shape the behavior in the desired direction. Once the task is learned and is being completed that performance should be reinforced every time. After a short period of reinforcing every successful effort the frequency of reinforcement should be gradually reduced. The final stage will consist of random reinforcement based on time intervals or the number of correct repetitions. The randomness of the reinforcement is essential to insure the behavior is consistent. The random reinforcement encourages continuous performance because the reinforcement may come at any time, but only if the task is completed correctly. Therefore, if the employees are to be rewarded they must continue to perform satisfactorily. It is very important that the reward not come immediately after the task is completed incorrectly, unless that is the action you want to encourage.

PUNISHMENT AND EXTINCTION

Reinforcement theory also includes two methods to reduce unwanted behaviors and actions. Punishment probably does not need much explanation since we all see it regularly and have experienced it at some point in our lives. Suffice it to say that any actions by managers perceived by employees as a negative consequence are punishment. So, what is extinction? The short answer is the elimination of unwanted behaviors by ignoring them, thereby providing no unintended reinforcement for them. If you have ever seen a parent walking along with a crying child and wondered why they are not responding to the child, you have seen an effort to extinguish a behavior. Employees, like the child just mentioned, will sometimes act in ways to gain attention. As mentioned in the discussion of reinforcement, sometimes any attention is better than no attention: especially if the employee is not getting the attention they need from the manager. If it seems like this discussion has gone full circle back to the earlier discussion of feedback, it has. Employees who receive feedback on their performance are less likely to act in unacceptable ways to get the attention of the manager.

Ignoring unwanted actions or behaviors is not always possible as a means to reducing the behavior. That is when punishment may become necessary.

TO DO LIST

- Make a list of the possible rewards you can use to reinforce employee behaviors and actions.
- Identify the behaviors you want to reinforce (increase frequency) and the behaviors you want to reduce/eliminate.
- Develop a schedule for reinforcement that will match the guidelines given above.
- Practice ignoring the unwanted behaviors and rewarding the desired ones and keep a log of your actions to check your success.
- Make a list of ways you can provide feedback (especially positive feedback) to your staff.
- Give feedback to every employee at least once per day. At the end of the day review your actions to confirm your success doing this task and that any negative feedback was balanced with positive feedback.

Chapter 7
How Do I Know They Are Doing a Good Job

The only way to truly judge whether an employee is doing a "good job" is to have a clear definition of what the job is and what level of performance is expected. The first step can be accomplished by knowing how to clearly define the duties and requirements of a job. The second is accomplished by knowing how to define clear and effective performance expectations. Whether one includes the performance expectations into the job description or defines them in a separate document is not as important as making sure both exist. This chapter will discuss writing job descriptions and performance standards as individual topics.

JOB DESCRIPTIONS

A job description should describe the duties, responsibilities, level of authority, and necessary or essential qualifications for each position in your organization. Where there are multiple positions that are essentially the same, one job description should be sufficient. For example, it may suffice to have one job description for all salespeople in your unit, or for all the secretaries in the organization. However, just because two or more positions have the same title, they may not have identical job descriptions. For example, it is possible to have salespeople who are "in house" do their customer contacts by phone and simultaneously have salespeople who are out of the office calling on major clients. It is also critical to remember that job descriptions are not static and evolve as jobs evolve and therefore need to be regularly reviewed and updated.

Job descriptions, in addition to providing job specifications, also facilitate recruitment and orientation of new employees, performance appraisal, and recruitment planning. Knowing what duties an employee holding a job is responsible for provides the foundation for evaluating whether they have successfully performed the job. In order to recruit properly qualified employees it is critical to know what they will be doing and what knowledge, skills, and abilities they will need. By clearly defining justifiable knowledge, skill, and ability requirements applicants can be evaluated against a set of standard criteria. Having a standard set of criteria defined in the job description will help reduce the potential for bias to enter the applicant review process. In other words, the job description is the guidebook for making decisions about job candidate qualifications, incumbents' performance on the job, and establishing the orientation and training plan for the job.

So, how are job descriptions developed? Job analysis is the process of gathering, documenting and analyzing information about jobs. The information gathered in the job analysis is used to develop the job description. Job analysis focuses on three dimensions of the job: content, requirements, and context. Job content describes the duties and activities. This description can be general in nature or very specific in describing the tasks and duties of the job. For example a job duty may be written generically when multiple positions have the same job title, such as a job description for secretaries having a statement like "prepares correspondence for review and signature of a supervisor." Duties are likely to be written more specifically when the job description describes a unique position such as the executive assistant for the CEO.

Job requirements are knowledge, skills, abilities, education, licenses, etc. that presumably provide an indication that a candidate for the job will be able to successfully perform the duties and activities of the job. It is important to ensure that the knowledge, skills and abilities defined as required for a job are actually necessary. An interesting case that points this out is the case of Dave Thomas, the founder of Wendy's. We are probably inclined to think that the CEO position in a large corporation requires a college degree, but Dave Thomas did not even have a high school diploma. He received a GED when he was already fifty years old. So, what knowledge, skills, and abilities does a CEO really need? Similar examples can be found in many industries and organizations of all sizes. Therefore, it is important to think in terms of what a person in a job needs to know, be able to do physically and mentally, and what skills, such as communication, creativity, etc. are required. This requirement has been made quite evident by the Americans With Disabilities Act which requires reasonable accommodations be made for people with disabilities if they are able to perform the "essential duties" of the job.

Job context includes the aspects of the job that identify the level of responsibility, the jobs supervised, who the position reports to, work conditions, and physical demands/requirements. Is the job performed outside in all weather conditions? Does the job require flexibility to work overtime? Does the person in the job supervise others? Does the person in the job make decisions independently? The possible questions to be asked to determine the context of the job are clearly too numerous to list. The important point here is that each job will be performed within some organizational context that must be understood by managers and employees. The information for each of these dimensions is obtained from numerous sources. The following sections will discuss some of the primary sources for information related to a job analysis. Other sources may be available and some of the ones discussed here may not be, depending on the particular organization.

Sources for job information include: organizational documents, incumbents, supervisors, co-workers, and outside experts. Organizational documents refers to any manuals, organizational policy statements or technical literature related to the job. Operations manuals, employee handbooks, standard operating procedures, and equipment operation manuals are just some of the typical organizational documents one can use to get information about jobs in the organization. These documents often will provide information like skills necessary to operate a piece of equipment or expectations for employees' productivity levels. Incumbents are the people currently doing the job who can provide information about what they actually do. A word of caution is in order here. Incumbents should be asked what the duties of job are supposed to be according to the current job description, as well as what they actually do. Also, actual observation will allow the analyst to reach his or her own conclusions about what the duties of the job are.

Co-workers and supervisors can provide information based on their observations of the incumbents and how the job fits into the larger work processes. That is, what actions, decisions, duties, etc. are needed from the job to allow the co-workers and supervisors to do their jobs? Outside experts are excellent sources of information pertaining to similar jobs in the industry or in similar organizations. Experts may also be used to conduct the job analysis. There is research to support the approach of having incumbents, supervisors and co-workers define the duties or task of the job and having impartial outside experts define the knowledge skills and abilities necessary to perform the job. That impartial party may well be the human resources office.

There are four techniques typically used to collect the data for job analyses. The first step is to review organizational documents for background information. Existing job analyses previously performed for the job, training materials, current job descriptions, operating manuals, employee handbooks and sources such as the Department of Labor's *Dictionary of Occupational Titles* are all good sources for this first step. Job performance observation is another useful technique, particularly for jobs involving physical action that are best understood by seeing them performed. Site observation of incumbents provides data on the interrelatedness of tasks, materials and equipment used in the job, typical work conditions, and the interdependence of the job relative to others in the organization. Site observations should be made at different times of the day and over a period of several days to be sure to gather a full understanding of what the incumbents in the job do. The fourth technique for gathering data is the interview. Interviews may be done in groups, or individually, as part of the site observation, or as a separate part of the analysis. The focus of the interviews is on the tasks and requirements of the job. Structured interviews with open-ended questions are particularly useful. For example, questions that ask the employee to describe a typical day on the job in terms of the tasks they do, the amount of time spent on each task, and how they decide what tasks to do at any given time will elicit a great deal of information that can confirm observational data.

Considerable time will be required to develop the questions for effective interviews.

Now that the data has been collected the job description can be written. The job description should identify the job title, the duties to be performed, and the knowledge, skills and abilities necessary to perform the duties of the job. In addition to education, experience, physical requirements, and knowledge required to do the job, the knowledge, skills and abilities section should identify any requirements for travel, flexibility to work overtime, professional licenses or certifications, and any other special requirements. The job description may also include additional information such as the work environment (outside, in an office, etc.) and the type and level of decision-making authority the incumbent will have. The important thing to remember is that the job description will be used to recruit new employees, provide guidance to existing employees about what they should be doing on a day-to-day basis, and be the foundation for the performance review process.

The duties should be stated in action terms when possible. For example, instead of "responsible for preparing correspondence independently," that statement can be written in action terms that would define the duties as tasks that are performed. Such a statement would be "Independently prepares correspondence." While this may seem to be a trivial semantic concern, consider the first statement of duties and ask yourself "does that mean the person in this job actually prepares the correspondence or is responsible for making sure it gets done?" Task statements written in action terms unambiguously make it clear what actions and/or duties the person in that job will perform. After all, what you are trying to do is describe what an employee in that job will do so you can observe whether they are doing it.

PERFORMANCE STANDARDS

Once the job description is written, and the duties of the job are clearly defined, performance expectations can be defined. Performance expectations are the standards by which each employee's performance will be measured, or gauged. Performance standards spell out the amount and quality of work expected. They may also address the manner in which the tasks are completed, especially in service sector jobs. There are four characteristics of good performance standards.

First, if they are going to be useful, the performance standards should be measurable. That does not necessarily mean they have to contain specific numbers or quantities. Standards can be measured by assessing whether they are met or not. For example, a standard for the job duty identified in the previous section may focus on the correspondence being completed within a specified time frame; it can clearly be determined that the task was or was not completed within the time frame. Another performance standard for the same job duty may well contain specific numerical measures. For instance, a standard could identify an expected level of accuracy in proofreading the correspondence by stating a realistic minimum number of mistakes that will be allowed. A statement such as "correspondence prepared by the incumbent contains no more than one error in information, spelling, and grammar per every ten pages."

That last example points to the second characteristic of good performance standards—they are realistic and attainable. Nobody is perfect! Performance standards that require perfection will never be met and are likely to lead to frustration, job dissatisfaction, and low morale because the employees will perceive the expectations as unattainable. If a standard is unattainable and merit raises or promotions are based on meeting/exceeding the defined standards, then the employee will never be eligible for a merit raise or promotion since they cannot meet the impossible standard. However, attainability should not be equated with easy or guaranteed. Goal setting theory has consistently shown challenging goals, or in this case standards, will lead to greater effort.

The third characteristic of good performance standards is their direct connection to organizational goals. Performance standards must relate to getting the tasks completed so the organization achieves its goals. For example, if a key organizational goal is excellent customer service, a performance standard such as "All telephone calls are answered by the third ring" makes sense because there is a clear and direct relationship between promptly answering customer calls and good customer service. If the organizational goal is to improve productivity, then performance standards that address productivity improvements are appropriate. It is important, however, to be sure that performance standards are not contradictory. For example, expecting well written and error free correspondence will require adequate time. Therefore, performance standards that simultaneously require well written and accurate correspondence and require it be done in too short a time frame will be at odds with each other. Remember the requirement for attainability.

Fourth, performance standards must be clearly, concisely, and precisely stated. The standards must be unambiguous and understood by the employee and the manager. If the previous three characteristics of performance standards are met, this fourth characteristic will typically be present. However, the manager and the employee need to review those standards to be sure they both have the same understanding. As suggested in the previous chapter on communication, even when something being communicated seems to be easily understood it may not be. Using the communication model in Chapter 3 and the suggestions provided in that chapter, the manager and the employee must ensure they are "on the same page" in their understanding and interpretation of the performance standards. While well-written standards should minimize the chance for misunderstanding by being concise, specific, and measurable, final confirmation that employees and manager have the same understanding should not be overlooked.

TO DO LIST

- Prepare a set of question to ask during a job analysis interview.
- Make a list of possible organizational sources of information that will be useful for job analysis.
- Practice observing employees doing their jobs. Be sure they know what you are doing and why you are doing it.
- Write a job description for one of the jobs in your department. Review the description with an incumbent and ask for their feedback about its accuracy and completeness.
- Develop a list of knowledge, skills and abilities for one of the jobs in your department and review them with your Human Resources department for feedback.
- Write performance standards for one job description in your department using the four characteristics discussed above.
- Review the performance standards just written with the incumbent and ask for his or her feedback, especially about the attainability, level of challenge presented, and the connection the standards have to organizational goals.

Chapter 8
Monitoring and Documenting Performance

Competent managers know how to monitor performance and how to document the performance of subordinates. Good documentation can make formal performance reviews easier and help overcome perceptual biases that can interfere with objective evaluations of employee performance. Objective recording of actions, behaviors, and work quality as it occurs provides managers with a clear record of an employee's performance over a period of time. This record can significantly reduce the reliance on memory alone to recall the performance level of subordinates when the manager has to formally evaluate that performance. This chapter will discuss perceptual bias in the context of monitoring performance as well as monitoring and keeping records of employee performance.

PERCEPTUAL BIAS

Our discussion of perceptual bias will focus on three concepts—defining perceptual bias, its origins, and its impact on our evaluation of employee performance. Perception is a process by which we organize and interpret the impressions left by the things we see, hear, touch, taste and smell. The interpretation is to give those impressions some meaning within a context. Perceptions are influenced by three factors—the situation, the perceiver, and the object or target. The situation includes the setting, time and circumstances of the observation. The perceiver is influenced by his or her attitudes, motives, interests, experiences, and expectations. Factors related to the target include motion, sounds, size, proximity, uniqueness, and similarity. For example, suppose you have a very hard working, productive, congenial employee (target) at work (the situation) and you conclude he is someone you want to keep around because your experience tells you (the perceiver) he is just the kind of employee you like. If you see that same employee later, in a bar (the situation), and that employee has had too much to drink (situation), and you have had bad personal experiences with people who drink too much, your perception of that employee will likely be very different. You have observed the target in action in different situations and perceived him differently. The only factors the observer can alter is the perceiver. By being aware of some of the obstacles to accurate perception the observer can attempt to change their behaviors, attitudes, and motives. That means that managers need to be well prepared to understand the possible influences on perception.

Bias is introduced into the perception because of our need to organize and interpret the data as we receive it. In order to carryout this organization and interpretation we use shortcuts that speed the process. For instance in the case above you rely on past experiences to help organize what you see and how you perceive it.   Those shortcuts are particularly useful in interpreting the impressions of people.

Our perception of people is different from inanimate objects in one critical way. We see people in action and make inferences from those actions or behaviors. As a result of these actions and behaviors our observations become subject to influence from our perceptions of the individual's reasons for acting the way we see them. Attribution theory suggests that the meaning we give to the individual behaviors we observe will influence the way we judge those individuals. In essence we try, using the three factors of distinctiveness, consensus, and consistency, to determine if the behaviors were caused by internal factors related to the individual or external factors in the environment or situation.

Distinctiveness refers to whether the behaviors are different in different situations. The focus is whether the behavior is unusual or typical. If the behavior is unusual we are more likely to attribute it to external causes.   For example, suppose an employee who is usually dependable and conscientious takes an extra long lunch without saying anything about it. That is an unusual behavior that a manager is likely to attribute to some external factor like getting stuck in traffic. Similarly, if an employee who is usually moody and argumentative acts that way during a conference with the manager, that manager is likely to attribute the behavior to internal factors—"that's just the way he is."

Consensus is when everyone faced with a similar situation behaves in a similar manner. For example, in the long lunch case above if everyone returned from lunch late we are probably going to attribute it to traffic, an external factor. If the moody and argumentative employee is acting the same way the other employees in the department act we are also likely to attribute it to an external factor like the work environment or the style of management.

Consistency is essentially the opposite of distinctiveness. If an employee is always late for work, the behavior is consistent and we are likely to attribute it to internal factors.

Interestingly, research suggests that people are more likely to underestimate the external influences on behaviors and overestimate the internal influences. This error is known as fundamental attribution error. It helps explain why a manager may attribute poor performance to an employee when the problem is actually caused by outdated equipment or lack of resources. Since our tendency is to underestimate the external influences we are naturally less likely to look for external factors that may explain what the manager observes as poor performance.

As mentioned earlier, shortcuts are also used to organize our impressions. One of these shortcuts is selective perception. Selective perception occurs when a characteristic of a person or object stands out, or is more often noticed. Because we are unable to observe everything around us we selectively perceive the things that stand out. Imagine an employee who makes a mistake and is reprimanded even though other employees have made the same error and received no reprimand. That scenario is quite plausible because the manager recognized the unusual nature of the mistake by an employee who is typically very accurate. The characteristic that the manager's perception was selectively based on was the employee's excellent work. Therefore, the mistake was more apparent in the reprimanded employee because it did not fit with previous perception. How is selective perception a shortcut in perception? Since we are not capable of observing everything, we select the things we observe as a result of our background, experiences, interests, and attitudes. As suggested by the example above, this kind of selective perception leads to erroneous interpretations. In this scenario the manager has unwittingly used a shortcut to reach a conclusion without fully considering all the facts.

The halo effect is another shortcut in our perceptual processes. The halo effect is when a single attribute, positive or negative, is the basis of our perception. Consider the following example. You have an employee who is always the first one to work and the last one to leave. Your perception is that he is a dedicated, hard-working, conscientious employee. However, upon recognizing that your perceptions may be influenced by the halo effect, you decide to do some quantitative measures of output and discover that the employee in question does not produce as much as other employees. The halo almost blinded you to the reality. As mentioned earlier, the halo effect works both ways. Suppose the employee in the previous example is typically the last one in and the first to leave. Your perception is likely to be negative. But, when you collect your quantitative data you discover that the seemingly poor employee is among the best producers in your unit. It is important to recognize the potential for the halo effect and be sure you have gathered as much performance information as possible.

Timing can have a lot of influence on our perceptions. The timing effect refers to the tendency to remember the most recent events and have our impressions from them influence our perception of employees and their performance. This bias is particularly difficult to avoid if you evaluate employee performance infrequently. Our memories of the actions and behaviors of every individual employee we supervise are, by their very nature, limited. We observe an action once or twice over a long period of time and that action is overwhelmed in our memory by many actions that occur many times over the same period of time. Multiplied by the number of employees you supervise it is easy to see how more recent events will push more distant events out of our active memory. The effect is that an employee who is usually very good at her job but makes a mistake the week before the performance review may be perceived less favorably than she deserves.

Perhaps the most widely recognized perceptual distortion is stereotyping. Stereotyping is assigning attributes to an individual because we have assigned the individual to a specific group. The attributes we believe are present in members of the group are now influencing our perception of the individual. Stereotyping obviously prevents us from really knowing the individual, thus biasing our perceptions.

The challenge for the manager is to reduce the influence of perceptual biases. Managers who maintain records of employee performance over time with many observations are more likely to be able to reduce perceptual biases and evaluate performance more objectively. The remainder of this chapter will discuss ways to monitor and document performance.

RECORD KEEPING

Reducing the potential for perceptual bias is a matter of making a full assessment of the employee's job performance. That full assessment will require information and data related to all aspects of the employee's performance on all aspects of his or her job. Trying to reconstruct the actions and behaviors of employees retroactively is a prescription for failure. The data and information must be collected concurrently with the actions or behaviors to which the information relates. In other words, you must make and record regular observations of employees' actions and behaviors. Recording the facts of the observations will provide a relatively objective record of what the employee did during the evaluation period. It is important, however, that the record of the observations be as free from interpretation as possible. For example, if you observe an employee arriving at work late three days in one week, make a note of that fact. There is not enough information to reach any conclusion, yet. If you notice that same employee working diligently and being very productive, make a record of that observation also. If you request a specific task be done, keep a record of the request including what was to be done, by whom, by when and whether it was completed satisfactorily. The cumulative effect of these notations will be a full record of the employee's performance over time. The performance of the employee who was late three days in one week, but is diligent and productive should be judged by all the information.

How should the records be kept? One way to make this task less onerous is to develop a system that you are comfortable with. You can use a checklist, you can look for certain things on certain days, you can make notes only when something unusual (positive and negative) occurs, or you can reflect on your observations at the end of the day and make a record of who accomplished what, etc. The important thing is that the records be kept over time and consistently. A sample of a tracking sheet is given below.

What should you keep a record of? The simple answer is all the actions, behaviors, accomplishments, and failures of each employee in your department. That, of course, is not realistic. Any manager who tries to keep an up to date record of everything his or her subordinates do will not get anything else accomplished. You need to have enough information to have a full picture of the employee's performance without interfering with your ability to do your job. Different kinds of jobs and different kinds of employees will dictate different answers to the question of how much information is enough. Highly qualified professionals will typically "do their job" at a high level of performance. Newly hired, unskilled, or minimally trained employees will typically need more monitoring of their performance until they have mastered the tasks and clearly understand the expectations of management.

Performance Discussion Worksheet

Name of Manager:
Name of Employee:
Date:

1. What was the purpose of the performance discussion?

2. If applicable, what performance strengths were discussed?

3. If applicable, what performance issues were discussed?

4. What decisions/agreements were made during this discussion?

It is essential to note here that the record you maintain of your observations is solely for the purpose of providing data for performance evaluation and reducing the chance for perceptual bias. Any records of official actions by management should always be maintained in the official personnel file of the employee. There should not be more than one personnel file. Your records are merely notes to refresh your memory of an employee's performance over a period of time.

TO DO LIST

- Observe one of your employees (preferably a relatively new one) at work and make a list of all the situational factors that could influence your interpretation of what you see.
- Make two lists of all the attributes of the above target that could, and did, influence your perceptions.
- Record the behaviors and actions you observed
- Identify ways in which the behaviors you observed were distinctive from or consistent with what you usually observe in the employee you observed.
- Make a list of the characteristics of the employee that standout. What did you notice first? Do those characteristics give you a positive or negative first impression?
- List the stereotypes you applied to the employee you observed. Be honest.
- Consider all the ways your responses to the above tasks could distort your perceptions of the employee and his or her work.
- Develop a personal system for recording your observations of employee performance.

Chapter 9
Reviewing Performance for Improvement and Development

In Chapter 8, tools and techniques for monitoring and documenting performance were given. By monitoring and documenting performance, a manager is prepared to have constructive conversations with an employee. By following the processes in Chapter 8, a manager should have the necessary information to provide specific and meaningful feedback to an employee.

In this chapter, will examine the following:

- The importance of ongoing feedback
- Assuring performance expectations are the same for people in the same job classification
- Improving performance through feedback
- Coaching for improved performance
- Summarizing performance – the performance review

IMPORTANCE OF ONGOING FEEDBACK

Ken Blanchard has called feedback *the breakfast of champions*. Following this analogy, feedback is one of the most effective tools a manager can use to promote a dialog with employees.

Most employees want to know how they are doing in their work. And most are welcoming of feedback, if given in the proper way. Think back to the previous chapter on motivation and documenting performance and how perceptions can form a reality in someone's mind: in this case a manager's. If it is true that perceptions can form realities, and that perception is reinforced from repeated behavior, then it indeed becomes a reality for that manager. If it becomes a reality for that manager, it can, and will, drive the behavior of that manager toward an employee. An example of that is, again, referring back to the previous chapter, an employee who consistently is late to work and leaves early. One conclusion mentioned previously is, it could be there is a specific cause that is external to the work environment. Regardless of the reason, if it becomes a concern of the manager, then a conversation with the employee can be productive. It can help the manager create a better understanding of the situation. The manager can learn of circumstances that were not previously known. This conversation can be helpful in creating a better understanding of the situation and any next steps if necessary. In other words, correct or alter an incorrect perception. While this example does not specifically speak to performance of a task or project, the same logic holds true.

To improve performance, there must be feedback. To give feedback that will be constructive and help the employee improve and grow in a position and within an organization, there must be an open communication with his/her manager. In many cases, this is much easier said, than done. For the manager, giving feedback that might not be positive might be the difficulty. Many will avoid giving feedback if criticism may be involved. Some managers may not be good at communicating in general and make the assumption if nothing is going wrong, then feedback is not necessary. Nothing can be further from the truth. Ask yourself how many times you have wondered if your own performance is satisfactory because you have received no feedback. No news is not always good news in that case.

Another factor that can help with feedback is the employee asking his/her manager for the feedback. Employees may avoid this conversation due to fear of what might be heard. Others may not feel comfortable approaching a manager to ask for the feedback.

Creating an environment that accepts open exchanges is an essential ingredient for giving feedback and having employees feel comfortable asking for it. This is something that should be developed early on with the manager/employee relationship. Starting early in this relationship and doing it as often as appropriate is a recipe for a success.

ASSURING EXPECTATIONS ARE THE SAME

A new manager may not initially be comfortable in getting work done through others. However, one of your measures of success will be how you do just that.

Knowing you, and those you supervise, are on the same page is an easy way to successfully get your work done through others. To get started, you may want to ask yourself, *what needs to happen for my area to be successful?* Determine what these are. For example, in a sales environment, a goal would be to increase sales by 10% from the previous year. Ask yourself, whom you need to do what to make that happen. Naturally, those on your team who do the direct sales would proportionately have to increase their volume from the previous year. But what about any support staff a manager may have? How will that staff contribute to the overall success of achieving a 10% increase from the previous year?

Getting on the same page is accomplished by establishing clear objectives for each person on your team. Using the department goal of a 10% increase in sales, determine what your team members need to accomplish to help reach that goal. Let's use the support staff as an example, since they may not have direct sales contact. An objective may be to "provide accurate (no errors) presentations to sales staff within agreed upon time frame in the current year." This clearly states what needs to be accomplished.

Setting objectives is a precise way of assuring you and your employees are on the same page as to what needs to happen to assure success. Writing the objectives may seem difficult at first, but with time, will become easier.

One method for writing objectives is the acronym known as SMART. This means each objective should be:

- Specific
- Measurable
- Attainable
- Results oriented
- Time Bound

Let's look at an objective and see how each of these applies. An example of an objective can be "make 10 cold calls per month in the current year (can be calendar or fiscal)." The **specific** is 10 cold calls. The **measurable** is the number of calls (10). The **attainable** is something that you must determine. You do want to set your staff up for success, not failure. However, you also want to challenge them to achieve at a high level; do not make the attainable so easy that it is necessarily guaranteed. **Results oriented** means completing the calls. Making 10 cold calls per month determines the result. Is it **time bound**? In this example, it is time bound in two areas. One is in the number of calls per month. The other is the end of the year.

The more you can establish what success looks like by writing SMART objectives, the easier it will be measure the success of your employees. A rule of thumb is *if you can't measure it, you can't manage it.*

During the course of the year, you may find that the 10 cold calls established may be too many or too few. The objectives are not written in stone. If you find there needs to be a mid-course adjustment, then meet with your employee and come to an agreement on what needs to change. It may just be a question of needing some resource like a better cell phone with wider coverage areas so he or she can make calls more easily while travelling.

Identifying what needs to be accomplished to ensure success by writing SMART objectives, reviewing them on an ongoing basis and modifying when necessary, assures you and your employee are on the same page. It also sets the foundation to giving feedback to improve and develop your employee.

IMPROVING PERFORMANCE THROUGH FEEDBACK

As mentioned earlier, *feedback is the breakfast of champions.* Giving feedback is a critical responsibility of being a good manager. Otherwise, how can you move people to achieve their own personal objectives and in turn, achieve your department's and organization's objectives?

One question often asked is when to give feedback. The answer is simple – immediately and regularly. To provide some room for interpretation it is immediately or as soon thereafter as possible.

Let's look at this by using the sales team example that we have used thus far. You accompany a member of your sales team on a call. It goes very well and you are pleased. The person was prepared, had all the necessary information to provide to the client, answered questions effectively and you feel confident you will get more business from this particular client.

So, when do you tell your employee about your observations of the call? Immediately, in the next week, when you can get around to it, or at the end of year review? The answer is quite simple—IMMEDIATELY. If you rode together to meet the client, have the conversation when you get in the car. Waiting until the next week, when you get around to it, or on the performance review is far too late. Your employee will be left wondering if they did a good job on the sales call from you perspective. Do not assume that he or she will know they did a good job because you do not offer any critique.

Another aspect of giving feedback, in addition to the when, is how. Do you give it in generalities or are you specific? Again, the answer is simple—BE SPECIFIC. Here is an opportunity to reinforce the behavior that you want in this employee. Remember reinforcement from a previous chapter? Using the same example, how can you give *specific* feedback? In the observation above, you felt your employee was well prepared. Tell him/her that. It may go something like, "*Joe, you were well prepared for this meeting. You had all the necessary information the client needed. I feel this made a very positive impression.*" The other aspect was your employee answered the client's questions well. Again, be specific. "*When the client asked you about ABC, you answered correctly and thoroughly. I felt the client was more than satisfied with the answer.*"

These are examples of immediate and specific feedback. Oftentimes supervisors think that if they come out of the meeting described above and say *good job* they have given feedback. That is nothing more than a compliment. Good job at what, the presentation, answering questions, just showing up? How is the employee to know? Remember to be as specific as possible.

Types of Feedback

We have looked at when to give feedback (IMMEDIATELY) and how (BE SPECIFIC). Now let's look at two types of feedback—we'll call them positive and constructive. *Positive feedback* is the good things—what went well, things the employee did that were effective, etc. The other type of feedback is constructive. What could have been done differently? The examples given in the previous paragraphs are examples of positive feedback. (i.e. being prepared, answering questions effectively, etc.). We should know that our experience as managers and educators tells us that positive feedback is given far too sparingly, especially when weighed against the amount and kind of constructive feedback

Using the same scenario of the sales call, let's take a look at an example of constructive feedback. The employee was well prepared. He/she had all the information prepared for the call. Questions were answered correctly and effectively. One thing you wish had been done differently was for the employee to ask about the client's need to increase their order from your company. You felt the timing was right given how well the call was going and how receptive the client was to everything that was discussed. The time to give this feedback is IMMEDIATELY and SPECIFICALLY. Perhaps when in the car leaving the sales call, after you have given the positive feedback, you could say something like, "*Joe, when you were reviewing the growth of the client's company, that may have been a good time to inquire about increased needs from us. It may not be as effective to ask about this later when on a follow up call or email. When to ask for the sale or increase in sales is crucial. I think that may have been a missed opportunity.*" This gives the employee the immediate and specific feedback to improve for next time.

Remembering the feedback you give is also important as a manager. You want to reinforce those behaviors you want to continue and work with the employees on those you would like to change. It is very difficult to remember the specifics of each of these conversations in your head.

At the end of Chapter 8 in the TO DO LIST was a suggestion to *develop a personal system for recording employee performance.* Feedback is something that can and should be recorded to retain your record of conversations with an employee. Not all feedback need be recorded. If you did that, you would never have time to do anything else. However, feedback that you feel is significant to an employee's development, or anything that concerns you or that may be part of a pattern of behavior, is a good idea to record. It allows you to be SPECIFIC, and jogs your memory later during performance reviews, about what happened at some earlier time in the review period. Recall the sample Performance Discussion Worksheet given in the previous chapter. A collection of several of those sheets, or anything you develop to give similar information, accumulated during the year will be very helpful during the performance review.

Developing a system for recording employee's performance is something for your own use. It is not information that would go in an employee's permanent personnel file. If you find that you are recording like behaviors that are not changing and feel the need to take it to the next level, then is the time to consult your human resources professional about next steps.

IMPROVEMENT THROUGH COACHING

Another tool that can be used in the development of employees is providing coaching.

What is the difference between feedback and coaching? Simply, feedback is something you provide on an activity that has already taken place. Coaching is something you give to an employee prior to the activity to help him/her be successful. If you think about a sports team, the coach is working with players to prepare them for a game. The coach is also giving feedback during and after the game on what went well and what needs to improve. This is after the fact. The coaching is before the fact. The feedback is during and after the fact.

Using the sales example, let's see how coaching can be used. The sales call has not yet taken place. Your employee is preparing for the call. The two of you meet to review the materials to be presented. The employee is having some challenges in how he/she wants to say something about a particular point. You listen to the dilemma the employee is having and give some pointers on how you think the meeting should go. That is coaching. You are helping your employee develop by giving him/her direction based on your experience on what has been successful.

Think of coaching as giving advice and sharing your wisdom. It is a development tool to help your employees grow and be more successful. As a manager, you should constantly coach your employees for their growth and development. In other words, training never ends; you should use the opportunities presented to you to develop employee skills further. The additional benefit is your employees' growth and development has a direct impact on the growth and development of your department, and in turn, the organization.

SUMMARIZING PERFORMANCE

Most organizations have an annual performance tool. It is typically used to assess an employee's performance over the past year. In many cases, it is also used to determine a salary increase.

When it is time to do the annual performance evaluation, there should be NO surprises. Why? Because, as a manager, you should have given feedback and coaching to your employees throughout the year, as has been discussed in this chapter. Not only is it the right thing to do for your employee, it also makes your job as the evaluator a lot easier. You should use the system you developed to keep records of your feedback and coaching conversations.

If your organization evaluates employees by objectives as discussed in this chapter, then the monitoring, tweaking if necessary, and feedback on these will be a basis of our assessment. Some organizations use the essential duties and responsibilities shown on the job description as the means to evaluate performance. If so, you should look to these duties and responsibilities as the basis for giving ongoing feedback and coaching throughout the year as well as the annual performance review.

The annual performance tool can come in many sizes and shapes. It can be a one page review. It can be a 10 page detailed document to assess a variety of indicators of an employee's performance. Regardless of what type of tool is used in your organization, you need to have the information (data) to accurately and fairly complete the review.

In completing the tool used by your organization, use the information you have acquired through ongoing conversations with your employees. It enables you to give an accurate and specific assessment that should not surprise the employee because they know what feedback they received throughout the year.

Organizations can have different approaches to how the annual performance review will be completed. Some will direct managers on how to complete it. Others may not have any required method in place. Here are some of the options:

- The manager completes and reviews with the employee.
- The manager completes one and the employee completes one and after discussion, it is integrated into one for the employee's record.
- The employee completes a self-evaluation, reviews it with the manager and consensus is reached on the final documentation.

There is no right or wrong method. Use what will be most effective within the parameters of your organization's guidelines for you and your employee. If you have any doubt about approaches, contact your human resources department for guidance.

Looking at the above options on how to complete a performance review, one may shy away from having the employee complete his or her own evaluation thinking that it will only be glowing. What has anecdotally been seen is that employees may tend to be harder on themselves in some aspects than the manager ever will be. If the option is available to you, it is something worth trying to test this theory.

When you do sit down with the employee for the annual discussion, like giving feedback and coaching, be specific. This discussion again should have NO surprises if the feedback and coaching has been done throughout the year. Unfortunately, this is not the case in many organizations. Oftentimes, the only discussion is on an annual basis. Do not let this be the case with you.

TO DO LIST

- Write objectives for the jobs in your department.
- Set criteria for success with your employees.
- Practice giving positive and constructive feedback using scenarios that fit your work environment. Be sure that it is specific and immediate.
- Ask a co-worker to role model giving feedback with you and ask them to give you feedback on how you did.
- Write a plan for assessing the criteria for success throughout the year for relevancy. Make adjustments as needed
- Keep records of feedback and coaching conversations in your files to recall clarity, dates, etc.

Chapter 10
What If the Employee Is Not Performing

Nobody typically wants to terminate an employee, but ongoing poor performance is not an acceptable alternative. In our litigious environment managers need to be able to defend their actions when they do terminate a subordinate's employment. Competent managers know what information they should have to justify their actions and, how and why such terminations should be conducted.

First we need to clarify the use of the word termination in the context of employment. There are two types of termination in the workplace—voluntary and involuntary. Voluntary termination occurs when an employee resigns from his or her employment. Usually the employee will give advance notice of their intent to leave the employment voluntarily according to company policy. Typically, two weeks notice is the minimum expected and longer notice is usually expected from professionals or managers. The second kind of termination is known as involuntary. Involuntary termination means the employee's employment is being terminated by the employer. Involuntary termination is the focus of this chapter.

Most states in the United States are "at will" states in terms of employment. The at-will concept is simple and states that employees are employed at the will of the employer. In other words, an employer can terminate employment at their will. They do not have to have a reason, so long as the termination is not discriminatory as to race, gender, age, national origin, etc. However, because of the potential for litigation, or requirements to pay unemployment to the former employee, many employers today have adopted the policy of terminating employment with cause. In other words, employees are fired only when sufficient cause exists to terminate the employment. Be sure you know your employer's policies and practices. This chapter assumes that involuntary terminations are only initiated with cause.

JUST CAUSE FOR TERMINATION

Just cause for termination is obviously a very subjective determination. In this section we will discuss some of the legitimate causes for termination, understanding that this list is not necessarily complete, nor applicable in all situations. Since each situation is different, **it is essential that your human resources office be involved in the decision to terminate an individual's employment.** Your human resources office is familiar with past practices and precedents, company policies, and the legal requirements to support a "with cause" involuntary termination of employment. All of the "just causes" discussed below assume your employer does not have policies or precedents to the contrary.

In most cases, a termination with cause will be the result of progressive discipline. Progressive discipline refers to the practice of giving employees warning notices that their performance is not satisfactory. The warnings typically result in increasingly severe repercussions. A program of progressive discipline may begin with a discussion with an employee about his or her performance. The second step may involve some form of written documentation of the poor performance in the personnel file. The written warning may be followed by suspension or termination if improvement is not made. At each step in the process, prior to termination, a corrective plan of action is developed and discussed. In other words, the employee receives increasingly more serious warnings of poor performance while also being coached, further trained, or otherwise guided by the supervisor to improve performance.

Gross Misconduct

Gross misconduct can be described as behaviors that are obviously, and fairly universally, recognized as inappropriate for the work place. These behaviors are typically considered significant enough to warrant immediate dismissal, without progressive discipline. Such behaviors include consuming, or being impaired by the consumption of, alcohol or illegal drugs while on the job. This category does not apply to someone who may have a drink with lunch as long as it is consumed off the premises of the job, unless their performance is impaired. Use of illegal drugs during work hours should never be accepted, even if they are consumed away from the job site. The guide for managerial action in a case of suspected substance abuse should be the employee's impairment, or inability to perform the duties of the job. However, if you, as a manager, personally witness drinking of alcohol or use of drugs then the requirement for impaired performance is unnecessary.

Other forms of gross misconduct are related to employee behaviors. Illegal activity, physical and verbal assault of fellow employees, morally inappropriate behaviors, blatant and reckless disregard for policies and procedures, intentional damage or destruction of employer property, threats of physical violence or harassment and intimidation of fellow employees may also be grounds for immediate termination for gross misconduct.

Poor performance

Poor performance is defined by the expectations of management. Those expectations should be made clear, be realistic, and be appropriate for the job and work situation. Progressive discipline is our recommended approach to dealing with poor performance. A rush to judgement about an employee's performance can mean unnecessary turnover and extra work for the manager and other employees. At the same time, the manager must balance the interests of the other employees and the employer in making a decision about how long to try to improve an employee's performance before taking steps to officially begin progressive discipline. New employees clearly should be given more leeway for errors and lower performance while they are learning the job. The challenge for the manager is carefully assessing whether the employee has received the necessary training, resources and supervisory support to realistically be expected to be performing at acceptable levels. Depending on the kind of job the learning curve may be long or short. The more complex the job is, the longer the learning period will be. However, the more highly qualified the employee is, the faster they should be able to master the new job. For professional positions the employee may need as much as six months to a year to be fully proficient in all aspects of the job. For routine jobs employees can be expected to maser the tasks much more quickly.

So, how does the manager make the judgement about whether an employee's performance is unsatisfactory? One way is to develop expectations based on the performance of current employees. What is the average length of employment of the employees doing a particular job? Describe the highest performance you observe in terms of behaviors, actions, attitude, speed, accuracy, or any other measures appropriate to the job. Describe the poorest performance of the satisfactory employees in the same way. From the descriptions develop expectations that are challenging, measurable, attainable, realistic, and time bound. Now you have a standard against which to measure performance. What is a realistic time to allow for someone new to the job to achieve that level of performance? Of the employees who have been on the job long enough to have met the expectations, who is not? What is needed to improve their performance—training, equipment or other resources, or motivation? Now you are in a position to judge if an employee's performance is unsatisfactory, and the possible causes. Unsatisfactory performance can be described in terms of errors made, time to perform tasks, attention to details, follow through with commitments or assignments, absenteeism, taking too much break time and lunch time, or other failures to meet the defined expectations. Your job as the manager now becomes one of rectifying the situation by improving the performance or, if necessary, terminating the employment.

CONDUCTING PROGRESSIVE DISCIPLINE

As noted earlier, progressive discipline is a process of increasingly severe consequences for poor performance. Each step in the process should be carefully documented and ensure the employee is informed of the potential results of continued poor performance. Progressive discipline usually begins with a performance conference. In this conference the manager will describe how the employee's performance is unsatisfactory giving specific examples.   Such conferences are sometimes called verbal warnings. The performance expectations should be reviewed and clarified. A plan of action for the employee should be developed and the employee and supervisor should agree on a time line for improvement. The plan of action will identify what the employee must do to illustrate his or her improvement and what the manager will do to facilitate that improvement. The employee may be required to review the job descriptions to refresh their memory about the job duties. The employee may have a plan for further training, or mentoring, or regular reporting on progress to the supervisor. The manager may need to do more training, commit to more coaching or closer oversight and increased feedback. The timeline for improvement should specify a time by which improvement will be clearly demonstrated. There should also be a clear statement by the supervisor of what the consequences of continued unacceptable performance will be—a written warning, a probationary period, termination, etc. The manager should maintain a record of the conversation and agreements regarding what will be done by whom and by when. A record should also be kept in the personnel file if required by Human Resources.   If the performance improves, the employee should be recognized and reinforced for his or her improvement in clear and unambiguous terms.

The typical next step in progressive discipline is often referred to as a written warning or probationary notice. Again, be sure to check with you Human Resource department for guidance on how to proceed if performance continues to be unsatisfactory. A written warning is similar to the verbal warning discussed above except everything is written down and an official record is maintained by Human Resources in the personnel file. This is usually the last step before termination unless your company has policies to the contrary. It is essential that an employee given a written warning is told in unequivocal terms that failure to improve performance will result in termination. A probationary notice is essentially a written warning that officially places the employment on a probationary status with a specific duration. This status is like that of new employees who are on probation for a period of time, during which, or at the end of which, their employment can be terminated without progressive discipline. When an employee is placed on probation it is typically with the understanding that employment can be terminated at any time if noticeable improvement in performance is not made. To be fair to employees, many employers require a detailed improvement plan to be developed for the employee to follow. That plan provides clear statements of expectations and benchmarks for improvement that define specific accomplishments that will be necessary for the employee to be considered to be making satisfactory improvement.

INVOLUNTARY TERMINATION OF EMPLOYMENT

If the progressive discipline rises to the point of termination there are legal and procedural issues to be considered. Under no circumstances should you involuntarily terminate a subordinate's employment without thorough consultation with your Human Resources department. They will provide you the guidance to be sure you have done whatever company policies require and that you have considered all other available options. The termination should be done in concert with staff from your Human Resources office to be sure your actions are consistent with company policies, precedents, and legal requirements.

A safe rule to follow for all disciplinary actions is "consult first, act second." Before you take an action that may create legal or morale problems and potentially disrupt your workplace, be absolutely certain you have the support of the Human Resources department and your supervisor.

TO DO LIST

- Check with your Human Resources department to obtain a copy of any policies related to progressive discipline, "employment at will," and definitions of gross misconduct or other bases for immediate termination.
- Review the personnel files of the employees you supervise. Particularly pay attention to past performance evaluations and any disciplinary actions.
- Write a set of performance expectations for each job in your department and review them with the Human Resources department for feedback.
- Ask your Human Resources department to help you "role play" a conference with an employee who is not performing satisfactorily.